TROUBLE-FREE TRAVEL WITH CHILDREN

HELPFUL HINTS FOR PARENTS *ON THE GO*

by
Vicki Lansky

illustrations by Jack Lindstrom

Book Peddlers • Deephaven, MN
*Book trade distribution by Publishers Group West
—in Canada by Monarch Books—*

Editors: David Smith, Kathryn Ring, Toni Burbank,
        Sandra L. Whelan, and Kate Moore.
Revised edition: Francie Paper

Special thanks to: Peggy Thomas, Pam Mueller,
        Colleen Finn, Mary McNamara, Peggy Markham,
        and Sherry Wood

Consultants:
        Neal Holton, M.D., International Travel Clinic,
            St. Paul-Ramsey Medical Center, St. Paul, MN
        Steve Frank, Minneapolis AAA Club
        Joy Sotolongo, American Academy of Pediatrics,
            Division of Public Education
        Dorothy Jordon, Travel with Your Children, NYC

Cover design: MacLean and Tuminelly
Illustrator: Jack Lindstrom

Special thanks to the parents who shared their words
and feelings. Most quotes are reprinted with permission
from *Vicki Lansky's* Practical Parenting™ newsletter.

The Book Peddlers
18326 Minnetonka Blvd
Deephaven, MN 55391
(612) 475-3527
fax: (612) 475-1505

96 97 98 99 6 5 4 3 2 1

Printed in the USA

CONTENTS

YES!
TAKE THEM AND GO

Travel with children is different from travel without them—no doubt about it. As you've discovered by now, they do change your life. And they will change the way you travel, but they don't have to prevent you from going out and about. The key to making your trip a good one for both you and your baby or toddler is careful planning, with your child uppermost in your mind.

Your own mental preparation is the first step. Your attitude will be the most important element of the trip. Learn to "expect the unexpected," and be prepared to change plans when a child becomes bored, overtired, or ill. And don't fantasize about reliving the "perfect trip" B.C. (*Before Children*). It's a myth. You can't, for example, just include a toddler in your spur-of-the-moment weekend jaunt or your tour of five Gothic cathedrals in one day.

If exploring new places to eat and sampling exotic foods have been important in trips B.C., be prepared to de-emphasize the eating experience. However much you've enjoyed casual travel and taking what the road offered, you'll find yourself making dinner reservations and phoning ahead. If you've loved moving from place to place as the inclination struck, you'll discover that children are more content when they're settled in at a home base and that constant packing and repacking with children is tedious. You'll want to slow down personally, too.

It may take you a few days to get into the travel mode with your kids. Not only will your child be tired at the end of the day, you also will be more tired than you were on B.C. trips.

Every family brings its angers, conflicts, and rivalries with them when they go on a trip. Being tired and hungry is how people often feel when they travel. Don't let that get in the way of having a wonderful time. When we look back on our lives, the times we really remember are those trips we take. They are our true memory-makers. Don't get bogged down in what really are little problems.

I enjoyed those trips with my children when they were young and I guess we had many of them. It's the only way I can explain their wanderlust today. Travel is what young adult children do today. They are citizens of the planet earth and have friends and connections around the world. E-mail addresses and computers have helped them keep in touch with far flung family and friends.

Computers today serve many purposes, including helping you find travel information. The Internet offers you new ways to access various kinds of information—from weather reports anywhere in the world to ordering free travel brochures to making your own plane reservations. I've tried to direct you to helpful cyberspace addresses that will add to smoother travel plans for your whole family.

Chapter One

PLANNING MAKES IT POSSIBLE

You can make your trip a wonderful adventure by using foresight and your best management skills. Keep your normal daily routines in mind as you plan for travel and for the days at your destination, allowing adequate time for rest and quiet as well as for active fun. Remember that you'll be living on CST—Children's Standard Time—and that a child's sense of time is different from yours. The uninterrupted six- or eight-hour drive that you find interesting and restful can be excruciating for a toddler, and the leisurely tours of shops you enjoy may turn into a "don't touch" sojourn of distasteful proportions for your child.

Perhaps the most important thing to remember is that from infancy through toddlerhood, children don't really understand the concept of travel and vacations. Every morning they wake to a new and exciting world; each day is different. They'll enjoy or not enjoy travel depending upon how they feel and what's going on at any given moment. Fatigue and hunger will be hardest on them—and therefore hardest on you. Tired children don't cope well.

Lastly, remember it is important to provide children with some unstructured play time each day when traveling.

Ages and Stages, Pros and Cons

What's the best time in a child's life to begin to travel as a family? As in just about every other parenting decision, there are advantages and disadvantages to every stage and phase. Get out your favorite child development book. Review all the things you can and can't expect from babies or toddlers your child's age, and apply them to the travel situations you'll experience.

Infants to 6 Months Old

A visit to relatives or friends (understanding ones!) may be your best bet for a first trip. Whatever you decide to do, try to keep it short and simple. The traveling life will be easiest for the nursing mother, who doesn't have to worry about bottles and formula and all the other accoutrements of bottle-feeding. Still, if you'll be abroad and you're nursing, it is wise to take some ready-to-feed formula with you "just in case."

Infants usually can be counted on to sleep a great deal, and even poor sleepers are likely to doze off more easily because of the sound and motion of whatever mode of transportation you choose. Should you have a wakeful baby, at least it's more fun to be bleary-eyed away from home. The excitement of the trip may produce that extra burst of adrenaline that will help you through trying moments. On the other hand, if you have an infant suffering from colic, it would be wise to put off any travel until your baby has passed that three-month point when colic usually dissipates.

Babies will spend most of their time sleeping on long plane and car rides. Packing, unpacking, and hauling around the extra amount of gear any baby needs may cause some tense moments. Still (especially if this is your first child), you and your spouse can both benefit from escaping the infant-dominated setting in which you've been living.

Babies of 6 to 12 Months

When your baby is about 6 months old, you'll probably enter a time of major change, which some call the *Rude Awakening*. Your passive baby is no longer passive. He or she is now old enough to know who you are and when you're gone, but not yet old enough to be sure you're coming back. Exploration begins in earnest, and you'll soon discover that your baby's hand is often quicker than your eye. Your baby's developing mobility now makes it impossible to turn your back on him or her, and you can no longer plan to make an infant's sleeping "nest" out of any convenient spot.

Although attention spans are short, it's usually not hard to entertain a baby this age, especially if you don't mind repetition. As one parent remarked, "If I never play *Pat-a-Cake* or *This Little Piggy* again, it will be too soon!"

Structure, when possible, will be your best tool for your child. Sticking as close as you can to bedtime routines, similar foods and your expectations for baby can help smooth out tense times.

On a relaxed vacation schedule, you may well have the pleasure of enjoying some of your baby's "firsts": crawling, walking, and—less thrilling—the emergence of new teeth.

Toddlers Ages 1 to 2

Toddlers' attention spans are slightly longer than those of babies, and you'll probably discover that you can find a few extra moments for yourself while your child is occupied with a toy or a snack. You'll enjoy watching your child's reactions to and amazement at new sights as well as the growing ability to express wonder and delight in words (yes, and demands and complaints, too). Delayed gratification means nothing at this age. When a toddler wants something, he or she wants it now! Toddlers are self-centered, often seeming to feel that adults were put on earth only to gratify their wishes. They are full of energy, easily frustrated and often fussy eaters.

You may want to avoid hotels if you feel your child might be a disturbance (day or night), choosing instead to stay with relatives or to rent a condo or house.

Toddlers require a lot of exercise, and you'll find frequent stops necessary if you're traveling by car. Your best trick will be sharpening your ability to anticipate your child's mood. If you can see hunger, frustration, boredom, or over-tiredness coming, you can stop and do something about it before it gets out of control. After an exercise break, your toddler may resist getting back in the car seat. You can make the transition easier by bringing out a new book or singing some good loud songs.

Grandma may be disappointed to find a child of 2 or so not as outgoing and loving as she might like. Strangers, even related ones, are welcomed by some children but not by others.

(Also, this is the final age airlines allow kids to fly free.)

Preschoolers ages 3 to 4

You will become all too familiar with "Are we there yet?" (*No!*) The positive side to this question is that there is much available to entertain your preschooler. The good news is that children in this age group are easily entertained by toys. The bad news is that you must carry a good supply with you. Better yet, bring some new toys as surprises.

Children 4 and up start to become real pleasures to travel with as they become more adventuresome and verbal.

Vacations shouldn't produce battles or enforced discipline that really won't prove anything. You should be able to enjoy your trip on your own terms. If others think you're spoiling your child (whatever that means), so be it.

And keep in mind that this is your vacation, too. You and your spouse may need some time alone to help you deal with this intense family time. Don't feel guilty about going off alone— separately or together—on occasion.

Ages 5 and up

Starting now, your travel times will most often be determined by your child's school schedule. Vacations get more expensive as you join the winter peak travel season times.

Children are now more independent and have better social skills. They will enjoy group interaction and babysitting clubs. They are also less burdensome to watch when they're near the water, so beach vacations become more relaxing.

Vacations can become learning adventures as children's horizons widen. Their food choices, however, will remain narrow for most kids despite their growing love for adventure.

From this age on, your vacations become permanent memories of family times for your child.

Ages 7 and up

Many adventure vacations allow children 6 or 7 and up to participate, including those now marketed to travel with grandparents. By this age, theme parks begin to be truly appreciated. A child's endurance is longer but you must still be prepared for food and bathroom stops.

Once children have hit the double-digits, they often don't want to leave their friends. Some families accommodate their kids by allowing friends to come along. Or they may pick vacation spots like Club Med or take cruises where there is a built-in peer group. At this age individual styles really do count.

If your children do not seem to have a sense of adventure, are not very accommodating or do not appreciate the joys of travel, then for the next few years — don't! Instead, take the type of trip you'd enjoy without them and find a middle-ground—long weekends or the special-interest vacations that interest them.

So Where are You Going?

Your travel plans will most likely revolve around what you and your spouse think you'd enjoy doing with your children. Time, money, and family obligations are part of that decision. The usual array of choices are:

Family/relatives visits	Camping-Cabins-Parks
Resorts/Theme parks	Learning vacations
Cruising	Ski trips
Farm/dude ranches	Adventure trips

• Send for travel information offered in newspaper travel sections. At the very least, your small child will enjoy looking at the photos with you and the chance to tear up the brochures. Older children will enjoy being part of the planning process.

• Check into the availability of activities that are especially geared to young children. Travel guides usually list them, or you can write to local chambers of commerce for other ideas. Look for places with children's programs. Even if your children don't use the program, you know there will be other children and families around.

• Look through any of a multitude of books that are geared for family travel. There are the *Frommer Family Guides* (Prentice Hall Travel Books) and *Places to Go With Children* (Chronicle Books), the *Fodor Books:Where Should We Take the Kids* and *The Family Adventure Guides* (Globe Pequot Press).

• Plan your outings with children first in mind and then the adults. It's also best to plan your trip to fit the needs of your youngest child. For example, you know that activities that will require standing in line for any length of time will not work for a child, no matter how terrific the attraction. And seeing the Grand Canyon will NOT be a memorable experience for a 2-year-old.

• Don't overlook the impromptu "mini-jaunt." How far can you go on just a tank of gas? What can you do for a day for $25? Explore one back road for an hour. Let the kids plan a jaunt within your given limitations.

• Be aware that visits to museums and galleries will be covered quickly if your children are too old to ride contentedly in front- or backpacks. Your toddler may be more interested in the steps to a museum than in the exhibits; allow time for him or her to explore such preferred wonders.

Family Travel Resources

Specialty Services:

Travel with Your Children (aka TWYCH)
40 Fifth Ave
New York, NY 10011
(212) 477-5524

A travel information center providing detailed information and various publications for many types of family vacations.

Family Travel Guides Catalogue
Carousel Press
P.O. Box 6061
Albany, CA 94706-0061
(510) 527-5849

A free 32-page catalog offers a wide selection of travel guides for here and abroad, games for kids, and hard-to-find books.

Vacations with Children
P.O. Box 67
Suffern, NY 10901
(800) 606-4892
(914) 532-4476

A catalog that offers a wide selection of travel books specifically directed to parents traveling with children.

Travel Agencies:

Many travel agencies specialize in booking family travel, including travel with grandparents. A few are listed here. Call for their brochures:

Vistatours/ Carson City, NV	(800) 248-4782
Families Welcome/Durham, NC	(800) 326-0724
Travelling With Children/Berkeley, CA	(800) 499-0929
Rascals in Paradise/San Francisco, CA	(800) U-RASCAL
Family Explorations/Swathmore,PA	(800) WE-GOTOO
Grandtravel/ Chevy Chase, MD	(800) 247-7651
Elderhostel/Grandchild Program	(617) 426-7788

Your Computer:

Some helpful sites on the Internet:
http://www.yahoo.com/recreation/travel
http://www.travelchannel.com
http://www.cntraveler.com
http://www.travelocity.com

• Check to see if the city you'll be visiting has a children's museum. They make wonderful outings. See page 142.

Theme Park Vacations

Visiting Disneyland and/or DisneyWorld has become almost a rite of passage for families today. Who dares admit they have not been there or are not going someday? But more importantly, everyone does enjoy them. They are well-managed and have spawned a world of theme parks.

Children under 5 can have a good time if you don't try to do it all. Those over 5 will remember and re-live the adventure for years to come.

A relaxed pace is more important than seeing everything. (*You won't anyway.*)

Do Your Homework

Study up before going. Researching books and brochures beforehand can help you decide your priorities and avoid crisscrossing the park.

• Guide books can help you gauge times per ride/attraction. Any of the following annually updated books are worth getting before you go: *Birnbaum's Official Guide to Disneyland* and *DisneyWorld*; *Birbaum's Walt DisneyWorld for Kids by Kids* (Hyperion); *Unoffical Guide to Disneyland* and *Walt DisneyWorld* (Prentice Hall) and *The Amusement Park Guide: Over 250 Amusement Parks from Coast to Coast* by Tim O'Brien (Globe Pequot).

• Internet addresses for more information:
http://www.disney.com/DisneyWorld/index.html
http://www.disney.com/Disneyland/index.html
http://www.mcs.net/~werner/links.html (links to Disney theme parks, hotels and attractions in US and abroad)

• Beat the odds. Go early—very early—even before the gates open. (Call the day before for opening and closing times; they sometimes change.)

• "Quiet" times (relatively speaking), are said to be in January, May, September and October and the first 2 weeks in December.

• Visit animal parks early in the morning as the animals are more lively at that time. Obey rules in safari parks.

• Discuss with your children what to do if you get separated. Be sure they know the name of their hotel, bus number, your first and last name (have practice sessions). Let them know that they may ask any park attendant to take them to the "Lost" area and that you will meet them there. (Also see page 82 about kid's ID bracelets.)

Time is of the Essence

• If your hotel sells tickets, buy them in advance to avoid long lines at the gate.

• If the line is short, get on it!— then ask what it's for! New rides tend to have the longest lines.

• Arrive at shows 15 to 30 minutes early to get good seats since kids enjoy shows more when they can sit up front.

• You'll save money (and time spent in long lines) if you avoid the Christmas or Easter vacation weeks.

Be Good to Yourself

• Eat lunch early. Attractions are quieter at lunch time.

• Dress comfortably. If you're going on wet rides, avoid wearing jeans. They dry slowly.

• Ask someone to hold your place in line if you need to walk with a fussy baby.

• Bring hats and sunscreen for hot afternoons.

• While standing in lines, have the kids quietly make up stories about the people around you, or take "surveys" of how many kids are in line or how many are wearing blue.

• Take an afternoon break. Have your hand stamped as you leave and then you can return in the evening.

• Pack a few small drinks and snacks in your bag. Even though you're not supposed to bring food into theme parks, a snack can help in needed times.

• Bring a stroller if you have a young child. It gives the child a chance to nap while you tour.

• Consider staying at hotels near the park. They are usually higher in price, but often offer shuttle services to the theme parks and save "commuting" time and parking fees.

Have You Wondered about Cruises?

Cruise vacations have become some of the best valued vacations for families, regardless of the age of your children.

Many have facilities and sitters for the very young but practically all have tons of activities for children of every age. Referred to as "offshore spoiling," parents and children alike seem to love cruise vacations. Package air/cruise fares make this a surprisingly affordable vacation when you realize that almost everything is included in the package price. Several lines offer children's programs only on specific cruises.

• Reserve early. If you book 3 months in advance you may get a substantial discount.

• The Caribbean and Mexico are nearby destinations with favorable weather (but do avoid the fall hurricane season).

• Be sure the children's program is designed for your children's ages.

• Be prepared to spend time with your child for the first day or two so he or she may adjust to the ship's program.

• Warn your kids about the very small size rooms. Don't spend much on rooms—you'll hardly ever be in them.

• Look for *Great Cruising Vacations with Your Kids* (World Leisure Publishing) by Dorothy Jordon from TWYCH. Call (212) 477-5524 for price information.

Club Med/All-inclusive Resort Vacations

Four Club Med locations offer all-inclusive vacations with Petit, Mini Clubs and Kids Clubs for children ages 2 to 11 years in the U.S., the Caribbean, and Mexico. (Two locations have baby clubs.) They also offer a Circus Workshop and a Kids' Tennis Program at many locations. At some of their clubs there are periods when children under age 5 can stay for free. This is generally into mid-June, then September through mid-December, but varies from club to club. They have changed their one-week vacation requirement to a flexi-vacation program. Some European Club Meds are also family-friendly, but English will probably not be the main language spoken.

For Club Med's latest brochure and current information, call (800) CLUB MED, or http://www.clubmed.com.

• Ask for a ground floor room when you arrive, and for adjoining rooms if you're booking more than one.

• Charter flights are not always on time. So be prepared.

It's still worth the price and inconvenience. (Keep swimsuits in your carry-on luggage in case your luggage arrives later.)

• Keep in mind the number of time zone changes you'll be making when picking a Club site. The more zones you cross, the longer it will take kids to adjust when you arrive—and when you return home.

Prefer to go Back to the Land?

Many families have discovered the enjoyment and quiet change of a weekend or week's vacation on a farm. Dude ranches can be another wonderful family vacation choice. *Farm, Ranch and Country Vacations* (Adventure Guides), (800) 252-7899 and *Ranch Vacations* by Gene Kilgore (John Muir Publications), (800) 285-4078 offer ideas for visiting rural America. The Dude Ranchers Association, (970)223-8440 offers a complete directory of vacation ranches in Western US and Canada.

Reservations & Accommodations

If this is your first trip with your child and you'll be staying in a hotel or motel, you'll probably be more comfortable at a family-oriented establishment. Travel agents can be especially helpful here, as will state-by-state guidebooks from bookstores, libraries, or the AAA.

• Make motel, hotel, or resort reservations as far ahead as possible, especially if you're traveling at the most popular vacation times.

• Always ask about accommodation amenities (especially swimming pool facilities and hours), and prices for children (they often stay free under the ages of 12 or 18 if they are in the same room). Many of the major chains offer special family rates, and most provide cribs free or at nominal fees. Some supply small refrigerators and/or laundry facilities.

Places to See Dinosaurs

Most children have a real fascination with dinosaurs. The following museums are just some of those which have excellent dinosaur exhibits that you might want to put on your itinerary—if you're within "stalking" distance.

American Museum of Natural History
New York City, NY
(212) 769-500

Peabody Museum of Natural History
Yale University
New Haven, CT
(203) 432-5050

Dinosaur State Park
Rocky Hill, CT
(203) 529-5816

Carnegie Museum of Natural History
Pittsburgh, PA
(412) 622-3131

National Museum Of Natural History
Washington, DC
(202) 357-2700

Natural History Museum
Cleveland, OH
(216) 231-4600

Dinosaur Valley State Park
Glen Rose, TX
(817) 897-4588

Fossil Butte National Monument
Kemmerer, WY
(307) 877-4455

Museum of the Rockies
Montana State Univ
Bozeman, MT
(406) 994-2251

Los Angeles County Museum of Natural History
Los Angeles, CA
(213) 744-3466

Page Museum of La Brea Discoveries
Los Angeles, CA
(213) 936-2230

Denver Museum of Natural History
Denver, CO
(303) 322-7009

Museum of Western Colorado
Grand Junction, CO
(303) 242-0971

Dinamation International Society
Grand Junction, CO
(800) 547-0503

Tyrell Museum of Paleontology
Alberta, Canada
(403) 823-7707

Din. Provincal Pk
Alberta, Canada
(403) 378-4342

Milwaukee Public Museum
Milwaukee, WI
(414) 278-2702

Field Museum of Natural History
Chicago, IL
(312) 922-9410

Petrified Forest National Park
Holbrook, AZ
(602) 524-6228

Triassic Park
Petrified Forest, AZ
(502) 524-6224

Dakota Dinosaur Museum
Dickson, ND
(701) 225-3466

Utah Field House Nat'l History State Park & Dinosaur Gardens
Vernal, UT
(801) 789-3799

Utah Museum of Natural History
U of Utah Campus
Salt Lake City, UT
(801) 581-4303

Dinosaur National Monument
Jensen, UT
(801) 789-2115

• Keep in mind that a motel on the outskirts of a town is more apt to offer play space and playground equipment than a downtown one.

• Stay at a place with a pool if you can afford it.

• Check your reservations; be sure any necessary deposits have been made and that rooms will be held for your arrival. You may wish to try the Hotel Reservation Network, a free discount hotel booking service. Call (800) 964-6835

Best Rooms to Request with Children

• Ask for a ground-level room in a motel to save hauling children and luggage up and down stairs.

• Consider two rooms, if your budget allows; everyone may sleep better. If you have two adults, book two rooms as singles with a child for each adult. You can save 25% to 40% on your room rates this way. Obviously, connecting rooms are best, but if that's not possible, you may want to bring along a room intercom. (See page 46.)

• Check into the possibility of a two-room suite (a bedroom and living room with convertible beds in the living room). The cost may be the same as, or even less than for two rooms.

• Ask if there is a special rate for adjoining rooms.

• Request the end two rooms in a section. If the children are at the end of a hall or near drink dispensers, laundries, or staircases, you will have less worry about the noise they most likely will make.

All-Suite Hotels

Some of the best accommodations for families are all-suite hotels that have kitchen facilities—enabling families to eat in (eating out is the most difficult expense to keep down when traveling). Since "all-suite" has become an "all-purpose" term, ask for a description of their suites or a brochure to be sent to you. (See page 132 for calling in Canada.)

Clubhouse	(800) CLUBINN
Courtyard (Marriott)	(800) 321-2211
Embassy Suites	(800) 362-2779
Guest Quarters	(800) 424-2900
Hilton Suites	(800) 445-8667
Homewood Suites	(800) 225-4543
Journey's End	(800) 668-4200
Marriott Residence Inns	(800)331-3131
Quality Suites	(800) 228-5150

Hotel/Motel Chains

Americann	(800) 634-3444	La Quinta	(800) 531-5900
Best Western	(800) 528-1234	Loews Hotels**	(800) 23-LOEWS
Budgetel Inn	(800) 428-3438	Motel 6	(505) 891-6161
Budget Host	(800) 283-4678	Marriott	(800) 228-9290
Clarion	(800) 424-6423	Omni	(800) 843-6664
Comfort Inn	(800) 424-6423	Park Inn Int'	(800) 437-7275
Days Inn	(800) 329-7466	Quality Inns	(800) 424-6423
Disney Resorts	(800) 444-8888	Radisson Hotel	(800) 333-3333
Econo Lodge	(800) 55-ECONO	Ramada Inns	(800) 272-6232
Exel Inn	(800) 356-8013	Red Roof Inns	(800) 843-7663
Family Inn	(800) 251-9752	Rodeway Inns	(800) 424-6423
Friendship Inns	(800) 424-6423	Sheraton	(800) 325-3535
Hampton Inns	(800) 426-7866	Signature Inn	(800) 822-5252
Hilton**	(800) 445-8667	Sleep Inn	(800) 424-6423
Holiday Inn**	(800) 465-4329	Sonesta Int'l	(800) SONESTA
Howard Johnson	(800) 446-4656	Stouffer	(800) 468-3571
Hyatt**	(800) 223-1234	Super 8 Motel	(800) 800-8000
Hospitality Int'l*	(800) 251-1962	Travelodge	(800) 578-7878
		Westin Hotels**	(800) 228-3000

* includes Scottish, Red Carpet, and Master Hosts Inns

**Offer Kids Cubs at certain locations. Call for details.*

Beyond Hotels and Motels

You may want to investigate the possibilities of villas, townhouses, cabins, or condominiums that offer comfort, privacy, and kitchen/laundry facilities. These home-away-from-home retreats can be ideal. Yards, separate bedrooms and a kitchen can create a relaxed atmosphere. Sharing one with another family also reduces your costs. Many of these list retreats in the Caribbean.

Hideaways International
767 Islington St.
Portsmouth, MA 03810
(800) 843-4433
    and:
Barclay International
Passports Ltd

Villas International
605 Market St. #510
S. Francisco CA 94105
(800) 221-2260

(800) 845-6636
(800) 331-6881

Condos

Although condominiums tend not to have organized activities for families, you will probably find them more economical than hotels. Just the money you save by making your own meals may make this option worthwhile. While condos can be booked through travel agents, you may wish to look into this yourself.

• Find out if a resident property manager works at the property you're renting or if he/she lives nearby.

• Ask about security deposits, check-in and -out times, and cancellation policies.

• Determine if linens, telephone service, and cleaning are included in the rental price.

• Look for the book, *Condo Vacations* by Pamela Lanier (Ten Speed Press) which lists over 3000 condos available for vacations.

Two agencies for condo rentals are:

Condominium Travel Assoc.   (203) 975-7714
Condo Club, Inc.   (800) 272-6636

Home Exchanging

Exchange houses or apartments with a family in another state, across the country or in another country for a comfortable home away from home. With the right match you'll save a lot of money, too.

If you want more information as to how this works, get a copy of *Home Exchange Vacationing* by Barbour (Rutledge Hill Press) at (800) 234-4234.

Vacation Exchange Club   (800) 638-3841
At Home Abroad   (212) 421-9165
Rent a Home International   (206) 545-6963
Interhome   (201) 882-6864
International Home Exchange (415) 435-3497

More information is available on the Internet from the web site http:// www.homexchange.com.

Home Rentals

Rent another family's home. Travel agents and tourist boards are good leads. There are also organizations to check with. When writing to the services listed, indicate the number of people in your party, the number of children and their ages, your price range, and any specialized interests you have.

At Home Abroad   (212) 421-9165
Villa Leisure   (800) 526-4244
Interhome   (201) 882-6864

Campus Lodging

During the summer, many types of student lodgings are available to families. These include apartments as well as dormitories. The following books will prove helpful in locating student housing both in the U.S. and worldwide: *The U.S. and Worldwide Travel Accommodations Guide* published by the Campus Travel Service (P.O. Box 8355, Newport Beach, CA 92660) lists 375 American colleges and universities that offer summer accommodations. Also listed are 94 YMCA's and 340 other sites around the world. Or look for *Peterson's Directory of College Accommodations* by Jay Norman.

American Youth Hostels sponsors 300 hostels in North America and 6,000 world wide. These are usually dormitory-style accommodations. Handbooks listing all hostel are available to members. For information call (212) 783-6161. Another resource to contact is Hostelling International at (800) 444-6111 or Family Hostel at (800) 733-9753.

On the Internet, go to web site: http://www.hostels.com/hostels/.

Bed & Breakfast

If you are interested in Bed & Breakfast accommodations, inform any place you contact that you will have a child (or children) with you. Some houses don't accept children for any number of reasons, ranging from the owner's personal preference to concern over the care of antique furnishings.

Realize, too, that this type of lodging will not offer you as much privacy as more conventional accommodations. Walls are often not soundproofed, making it more difficult if you have a baby or young children.

Bookstores, travel agencies or libraries have a variety of guides to area-specific Bed & Breakfast accommodations.

Preparing the Family

Taking a weekend "practice run" is good preparation for an extended trip. You'll find that the planning, packing, and traveling exercises will be helpful when you undertake the real thing, and you will get an idea of how things will work on the longer trip.

There is little you can do to prepare a baby for travel, other than keeping yourself organized and seeing that your baby is clean, fed, and rested before you set out. It is possible, though, to prepare a toddler for a trip.

> *When our son was a year old, we went to California. We tried to compromise by doing the kidstuff in the morning and the adultstuff later in the day. Then if he slept through it, he didn't miss much.*
>
> Joan Grunberg, Chicago, IL

Special for Toddlers

• Use toys as props for your explanations. With a big map and a tiny car or airplane, show how you'll cover the distance "from here to way over there".

• Visit an airport or train depot, if you'll be using either of those modes of travel, so your child can become familiar with the noise and activity of departure and the sight of a real plane or train.

• Discuss time and distance with a child who's old enough to understand. Children's travel experiences often are limited to trips to the store, and the idea of days and nights away from home may be confusing. A daily countdown can be easy to understand if you make a paper chain and break one loop each day as you get closer to departure day.

• If you're visiting friends or relatives, talk about the people you'll see. Get out the photo album and let your child look at their pictures.

Arranging for Babysitters

By the time you reach your destination, you and your spouse may be more than ready for a night (or an afternoon) out on the town away from the kids. Some family-oriented hotels, motels, and resorts have off-duty staff members available for sitting. Most front desks or concierges will provide you with lists of recommended sitters. You may even be able to get your hotel's cooperation in arranging for a sitter before you arrive. Rates vary according to locale, and you will probably be responsible for providing transportation.

Working parents, who sometimes must be away for a day or two at a time, have discovered that occasional travel with a child provides quality time that's otherwise hard to come by.

Many believe it's just best to start traveling with your baby early on so they get used to it. Daytime sitters can be arranged for working parents ahead of time (the better the hotel, the better your chances will be) so parent and child can have a late afternoon excursion and dinner together. Remember, it's not selfish to ask for some space—physically or emotionally—for yourself (or selves) when traveling.

Not every place will have or recommend sitters, but well-traveled parents have devised other ways to locate one:

• Look in the Yellow Pages under "Babysitters," "Child Care", or "Sitters" to find a listing of agencies. These sitters are carefully screened; some are insured and bonded. Rates are higher because an agency is involved.

• Call a church or daycare center and ask for suggestions for reliable, qualified sitters.

• Call a high school, hospital nursing school, or business school. Many schools post part-time jobs as a service to their students. Ask for at least one reference and always check it out.

• Be open to asking local parents you meet (if necessary, go out of your way to do so) for names of reliable sitters in their locale.

• Look for fellow family-travelers with teenagers. These teens often are happy to earn a little vacation spending money by babysitting.

• Consider taking a teenage sitter with you, if your budget allows, to help entertain your child or children and to give the adults a chance to get away occasionally. Many teens are delighted with the idea of a trip. Your main expense for the teen will be for food and lodging. Be sure your sitter knows exactly what constitutes work time versus his or her own private time.

Since they were born, I've taken my children on various business trips to condition them to travel and the business world. Business associates usually have daycare or sitters to recommend. I'm able to stay out on the road longer, and the children realize trips are normal events that one leaves on and returns from.
Susan DeNuccio, North Oaks, MN

A Little Preventive Medicine

The last thing you need or want on a vacation is a child who doesn't feel well. Many problems can be prevented if you think and plan ahead.

• Be wary of your child's contacts for two weeks or so before you leave. You don't want anyone to be exposed to even a cold, yourself included.

• Don't schedule vaccinations or immunizations just prior to your trip. Babies often have reactions that disturb their eating and sleeping—which you will not want to add to your list of concerns.

• Schedule medical checkups for the children before you

go, if you suspect anything at all not normal. Seeing a doctor is especially important if you'll be flying, since even a slight cold or ear infection may cause a child severe ear pain when cabin air pressure changes during takeoffs and landings.

• Consider carrying or buying bottled water for drinking and mixing with formula. Even good-quality drinking water can cause stomach upsets in small children, simply because it is different from what their systems are used to.

• If you are switching to disposable diapers in anticipation of your trip, do so well in advance to see if there is a skin sensitivity to any specific brand.

If your child does get sick away from home, don't hesitate to call your own physician long distance (unless you're out of the country). It can be easier than trying to line up a new doctor. Many parents simply assume illness will occur during travel and pack accordingly.

One problem you may encounter is diarrhea, especially if you are traveling out of the country. You don't have to travel far afield for it to occur. Diarrhea can be caused by changes in drinking water, new or unusual foods, changes in routine, or simply the excitement of a trip. (See page 126 for more on the prevention and treatment of diarrhea.)

Planning for Tomorrow's Weather

For detailed weather information and one-day forecasts
for 900 cities (cost is less than one dollar per minute):
900-WEATHER (sponsored by the Weather Channel)
900-555-5555 (sponsored by USA Today)
To check weather reports online:
http://www.usatoday.com/weather/wfront.htm.
http://cnn.com/WEATHER/index.html.

On Your Way Out the Door

Make coming home as pleasant as leaving home. Be sure to have some meals in the freezer, buy fresh milk before you leave if your trip is a short one (or freeze your left-over milk) and be sure there are clean diapers awaiting you, and enough food on hand so you don't have to run out to the store immediately upon your return home.

Before leaving your house, check that:

- Your phone answering machine is on.

- Any timers for lights and radios are activated.

- You've run your garbage disposal so that it's clean.

- Perishables are tossed, the kitchen is clean, and all garbage has been taken out.

- Your thermostat is lowered (or raised accordingly).

- Your mail and newspapers won't be piling up.

- A neighbor or family member has a key and knows your whereabouts.

- Appliances sensitive to power surges like computers, microwaves and television sets are unplugged.

- Your doors and windows are securely locked.

- Check yourself for tickets, cash, credit cards, passports and confirmations!

Chapter Two

PACKING

When you travel with children, having the right equipment with you can make the difference between a great trip and a so-so one. The trick is to take just enough to cover your needs, but not so much that you can't carry it conveniently. Some things you can do without, and if you can't fit something in (or if you forget it), you can probably buy it at your destination. Better yet, rent it! So you'll do a little more laundry while away. That's okay.

If possible, don't carry a purse. Wear a fanny pack. Wear a backpack (even the one you use to hold a child can hold your necessities or packages). Split the load with your spouse!

Lighten your load by shipping gifts ahead to yourself at your destination. If someone will be accepting the delivery, write "Do Not Open" or "Hold for Arrival" on the packages.

Packing for Baby

If you were surprised to find how much equipment your new infant needed at home, you may be surprised again to find how much of it is essential when you travel, even for a weekend. Diapers come to mind first, and obviously disposables are easiest. There's more, though. Lots more to bring: all the little clothes, the feeding paraphernalia, the absolutely basic equipment and all those things it would be nice to have with you.

Basic Baby Baggage

Your baby bag—that ubiquitous carry-a~~ll~~ waterproof lining and a shoulder strap. If you ch~~oose~~ and pack it right, it will serve for everything from~~ ~~ extended vacation travel. Some baby bags come wit~~h~~ extends and can be used as a changing pad.

If fashion isn't important to you, a backpack makes ~~a v~~ery practical baby bag.

Minimum *Carry-all* Inventory

- Disposable or cloth diapers (one to four).
- Disposable wipes or tissues (or dampened paper towel/washcloth kept in a re-sealable plastic bag).
- Sample-size containers of powder, cream, lotion, and other necessities.
- Extra pacifier (if child is attached!).
- Food, formula, water, and/or juice (with appropriate extra bottles and nipples).
- Change of clothes (one to three).
- Bib or cloth diaper for cover-up.
- Plastic bags for disposables or laundry and extra zipper locking bags of various sizes.
- The versatile, all-purpose baby blanket.*

* The versatile, all-purpose baby blanket can be used: as a changing pad, to create a spot for napping, as a "lovey," as a nursing cover-up. as a coverlet for a crib away from home, folded for a baby's head rest, to pad a car or infant seat; and as a good "floor area" for baby play.

- To prevent leaks, pack medicines, toiletries, and liquid vitamins in re-sealable plastic bags before putting them in your baby bag.

• Keep a two-foot square of plastic or vinyl (or even a square of washable wallpaper) in your bag to place under your baby for diaper changes. You can buy commercial changing pads for this purpose, too.

• Consider packing a small snack for yourself as a quick energy booster. Baby isn't the only one to think of!

Always keep your baby bag stocked and ready to go. Don't wait until you need it. This way you'll always be ready to take off—a very free feeling.

A roll of plastic sandwich bags in the diaper bag comes in handy for everything from a wet diaper to a sandwich. I always forget to replace a bread bag or other single plastic bag, but the roll is always there—a real lifesaver!
Susan Miller, Wyoming, MI

Warm and Cozy
• Take stretch suits that cover a baby from neck to toe. They're compact, they rinse out easily, and they afford protection from sun and insects.

• Use blanket sleepers for nighttime and forget about blankets.

• Or bring along a big beach towel to double as a blanket.

Luggage Logic
For longer trips, you'll need more than a baby bag, of course. Don't just toss things into suitcases and duffel bags. Where you pack things can be almost as important as what you pack. If something isn't available when you need it, it's almost as bad as not having it at all. A snack in the cooler at the bottom

of your car trunk does no one any good if you are on an interstate highway and can't stop.

• Remove disposable diapers from boxes and stash them in the corners of suitcases or tote bags if you are trying to cut down on luggage.

• Plan on taking not less than three complete outfits, even if you're traveling light: one to wear, one in the laundry, one in reserve.

• Put your baby's clothes on top of yours if you are sharing a suitcase. They'll be easier to reach.

• Pack all the baby clothes in one suitcase. Keep outfits—T-shirt, pants, shirt, and socks—together to save time when you need a change of clothes. If you're really organized, you could pack each outfit in its own plastic bag.

• Line your suitcase with plastic garbage bags, which will keep your clothes free from outside moisture and provide you with bags that will come in handy for everything from packing laundry to lining bed mattresses. (*Warning*: Never let children play with plastic bags. They can be dangerous and cause suffocation.)

• Use nylon duffel bags for wet or soiled diapers, as well as for wet clothes and laundry. The duffel bag can be washed with the load of clothes.

• Packing disposable diapers in an extra suitcase will give you an empty one in which to carry home your purchases.

Basic Baby Equipment for Travel

A car seat that can double as an infant seat (never the reverse!). See page 98 for information on car seats acceptable for airplane travel.

A soft front- or back-carrier or a hip-sling. Look for a style that fits your taste, budget, and life-style. They are wonderful for traveling with infants and can be used at home in a variety of situations.

A collapsible stroller. The umbrella style is the lightest and most convenient and can be used by a baby not yet able to sit up. If you don't own one, surely a friend will lend you one for a trip. Many new ones have optional features (such as a windguard) that may be of interest to you.

A hard-frame backpack carrier. Suitable only for babies about 6 months and older because good back and neck control are required. They can be used somewhat earlier if you pad and support the baby with blankets or towels. Some have "loading" frames that allow them to be used (with caution) as feeding chairs or stand-up sleepers.

Using Your Backpack to Best Advantage
• Practice with your backpack before you go on any extended trip so both you and your baby find your comfort and endurance level. Comfort level for baby and adult should be at least up to an hour or it's not worth taking. Also make sure your baby will be comfortable falling asleep in the backpack.

• Wrap pipe insulation around the frame of a backp. make it more comfortable to wear.

• If your pack doesn't have a special compartment, you can still stash spare disposable diapers under baby's bottom.

• Carry a small mirror in your pocket to use as a "rear-view mirror" to check on your baby.

What you take, beyond the bare necessities, will depend on how you travel (obviously a car will allow you to tote more than a plane will), how old your child is, and how willing you and your spouse are to carry extra paraphernalia. Many parents say that less is better, despite the fact that there is comfort in being well-equipped. Other items to consider are:

- Portable carrying bed
- Lambskin rug
- Portable, collapsible crib
- Portable hanging high chair (see page 60)
- Walker that can double as a high chair
- Baby-food grinder (many consider this item mandatory)
- A plastic tablecloth can act as a bed protector, changing pad, under-the-seat dropcloth, etc.
- Thermos (wide-mouth is most useful)
- Room intercom
- A clip-on reading light. It can double as a night light or for finding items in the car when it's dark.

**If you are going by car,
pack the car the night before
or at least when the kids are somewhere else!**

Your Toddler

;rything you need for an infant and you'll be
e minimum of your toddler's needs. These often
rs get wetter and dirtier than babies, so they need
They get hungrier, so they need frequent snacks
anu ..   .nd they need the distractions that toys, books, and
games often. If you've passed the early stages of potty training,
you may need fewer diapers, but you'll probably have some
alternate gear to tote.

Additional Take-along Items

___ Clip clothespins for attaching clothes to hangers
or to drip-dry clothes overnight.
___ Mild soap and baby shampoo. You can use the
shampoo for hand laundry, too.
___ A flashlight and/or matches and candles.
___ A night light to make getting up in the night easier
and so your child can see where he or she is during
the night.
___ An extension cord—locations of hotel outlets are not
always convenient.
___ An electric fry pan or hot pot for quick meals in your
room.
___ A can opener, a paring knife, and a bottle opener
(or just a Swiss Army knife).
___ A small sewing kit and scissors.
___ A roll of masking tape to repair disposable diapers.
___ A plastic laundry basket to hold anything and
everything (as well as acting as a bath tub "holding"
seat for a baby).

And don't forget your camera and lots of film!

• Keep nonperishable finger foods on hand for hunger, teething relief, or distraction.

• Take childproofing equipment such as electrical-outlet covers if you'll be staying at a hotel or in the home of someone who might not have them.

• Take a new toy, however small. A vital aspect for entertainment is its being new to the user. Buy one or more in advance of the trip and keep it out of sight until you're en route. This is true for children of all ages.

• Maybe a "wrist leash" or harness to use when necessary.

• Bring a high chair strap (or carry an elastic belt to use as one) to keep a "climber" in place while eating out.

Clothing Considerations

• Select travel clothing with an eye to layering so you'll be prepared for sudden changes in the weather. Sweaters can be an important item. Make easy washability the main consideration when choosing clothes, and choose clothes that don't show dirt.

• Speaking of dirt, carry a stain remover stick in your diaper or travel bag, so you can apply it to fresh stains before they set when you know you can't launder right away!

• Pack by *rolling* each day's outfit for each child together. These can then be banded or slipped into a plastic bag and marked with the child's name. (You may also wish to pack everyones' pj's or swimsuits together as you usually will be using them at the same time.)

• To protect clean clothes, place packed shoes *inside* a pair of socks that will be worn by your child.

31

• Consider packing extra shoelaces for your child's shoes in case one gets lost or broken.

The "Good Trip" Fairy

Don't leave your sense of humor, your surprises or your warm fuzzies at home. Make them part of the trip. Who knows where the Vacation Bug will next deposit a surprise gift, the Munch Monster will leave a snack, or the Travel Trickster may leave a silly note. Love notes are enjoyed on vacations as well as at home! So pocket a pad of self-stick notes, a few little fun items and your imagination—and the *G.T.Fairy*!

Specials for the Newly Potty Trained

Some children are entranced with the idea of using unfamiliar toilet facilities; others find them scary. If you know you'll be traveling, it's a good idea to encourage use of unfamiliar facilities whenever you are out and about. Don't be surprised or upset if your child starts to have accidents. Go back to diapers for nighttime or even daytime use if your child regresses. Revert to disposables for now; relax and enjoy your trip. Don't make your trip a training battleground. Worry it when you get back home.

• Take a portable potty seat or a toilet-seat adapter of your choosing along when traveling. One excellent plastic adapter that folds down to a 6+" square that fits in your purse is available from Practical Parenting for $9.95 plus postage/handling. To order, call 800-255-3379. (See page 138)

• Consider keeping your potty chair in the car, or take a portable camping potty to eliminate the need to find a rest room.

• Let little boys use a jar or can for urinating in the car. A

plastic ice-cream bucket can work for little girls
good "fit." Always pull over for potty stops. (Co
fitted tops—once filled—are crucial.)

• Use a disposable diaper inside a larger plas
boy urinating. Twist-tie shut and dispose of it a҆   ̩ next
opportunity.

• Pack a waterproof sheet, small plastic tablecloth, heavy
plastic bag to cover mattresses, or a rubber-backed bathroom
rug that rolls up easily for travel. Hotel staff will be just as
appreciative as relatives and friends. Remember, diapers have
been known to leak (*and so have toilet trained toddlers!*).

"Ounce of Prevention" Checklist

• Your own first-aid kit (you can turn an old lunch
box into one), complete with bandages, adhesive
tape, sterilized pads, antiseptic cream, diaper rash
ointment, any prescription medications and the
prescriptions for them, rectal thermometer and
petroleum jelly, a nasal aspirator for the flu season,
syrup of ipecac (to induce vomiting in case of
poisoning, but ALWAYS contact the local Poison
Center before administering), baby acetaminophen
(such as Tylenol) or baby aspirin, and a first-aid
book/favorite baby-care book.
• Insect repellent, lip protection and/or sunscreen.
• Tweezers and needle for the inevitable splinter.
• The phone number of your pediatrician or family
doctor and pharmacy.
• Don't leave medication in checked baggage.
• Your medical insurance card.
• Adult acetaminophen or aspirin for you...since
traveling with little ones can have its trying moments!

Chapter Three

ENTERTAINING "THE TROOPS"

Infants don't need the distractions of toys, but infancy soon passes, and you find yourself taking toys as well as tots. Older children will want to pick their own favorites to travel with. This is a good idea, within reason, but don't rely on a child to pick the most appropriate toys. Let him or her select some favorites and choose the rest yourself. Don't let your toddler persuade you to take along a talking or musical toy. Any repetitive sound in close quarters will quickly drive all within earshot up the wall. Avoid truly treasured toys (they often get lost), expensive toys (they break, too) and those with LOTS of pieces (unless, a few more or less, don't matter.)

> **Remember that you will always be**
> **your child's favorite toy.**

Travel Toys, *aka Sanity Savers*

The smaller the toys, the more variety you'll have room for. Yet "small" can be a choking hazard for your very young

child. Also, small toys are more easily lost, drop┐
in tight places.

Consider preparing three bags of toys: one for t┐
for your destination, and one for the trip home.

Many cities now have toy libraries. If you cannot fin┐
information in your phone book, you can call your local lib┐ ┌y
branch.

• Bring suction cup toys, plastic keys or activity cubes for babies.

• Include soft toys to hug, cuddle, and sleep with. If you attach an elastic loop to a soft toy, a child can carry it on the wrist. (If necessary, you can wear it on YOUR wrist).

• Bring along Bristle Blocks or other large-size, snap together plastic construction toys. If you lose one or two, it won't be a big loss.

• Make a surprise package by wrapping several toys and books with lots of string and tape. Let your child select one when things get tense.

• Pack a special surprise bag for each child and fill it with surprises and special favorites. An old attache case makes a good carrying case as does an old purse filled with jewelry, a small brush, an old wallet, etc.

• Bring hand puppets to entertain a child when restlessness sets in. A puppet "eating" a small, deflated balloon looks as if it is blowing bubbles.

• Carry only WASHABLE markers with you. Be cautious with crayons. They can—and do—melt in the heat of summer.

• Blowing up balloons can provide good entertainment if there's an extra adult in the car. Keep them small, or let the air whistle out, draw faces on the balloons, tie one to a car seat. (Never let a child chew on broken pieces of balloons because

...here are chemicals on the inside of the pieces, and the pieces can also cause choking or asphyxiation.)

• Keep a supply of colored-dot-stickers-with-pictures on hand. They are fairly neat and really keep kids occupied.

• Consider buying travel-size versions of board games. Especially those that come with magnetized boards or pieces. Or use waterproof markers to trace your kids' favorite board game on a piece of clear, heavy plastic that can be rolled up and taken with you.

• Store small toys in a metal Band-Aid box.

• For kids hooked on video games, hand-held versions may well be worth the investment. Generally a good travel toy.

About two weeks before a trip I hide some favorite toys and even buy a few new ones. When boredom sets in, I give my son a "surprise" to open.
                    Wendy Lazear, Long Lake, MN

• Don't forget a Magic Slate! It can provide hours of fun with no mess and eliminates the need for excess paper. It probably will get ripped along the way, but then it will be one less thing to carry home. Also MagnaDoodle.

• Look for Mrs. Grossman's sticker kits to suit any age and interest.!

• Let a child (who is old enough) be responsible for packing a small backpack that can hold travel toys. The basic rule is your child can bring only what he or she can carry.

• Stock up on MAD LIB fill-in-the-blank game pads.

• Or bring new issues of children's magazines.

• Pack a glue stick.

• Consider swapping some old toys with a friend or neighbor or borrowing some so you'll have a few that are really new to your children.

• Teach kids a new skill such as knitting or buy small leather craft kits for them to put together.

• Use this time to let the kids help write down your family tree and family oral biographies.

• Bring along some paint-with-water books and a plastic bag filled with wet cotton swabs.

• Help kids select compact toys such as a deck of cards, puzzles in frames or pipe cleaners.

• A camera—even the disposable kind—is good for children to take along. Let *them* document the trip.

• Create an activity kit by punching holes across the bottom of several heavy duty, resealable ziptop plastic bags and put them in a 3-ring binder. Fill each "bag" page with art supplies or toys.

• Mount your map on a piece of foam core board, cover it with a clear laminate sheet. Now you can track your route with a washable or permanent marker and keep your map intact.

• Above all, carry books, books, and more books to read to your child while you're traveling, while you're waiting in restaurants, and before bedtime.

A Child's Travel Library

Whether it's *Madeleine* or *Babar* in Paris, or *Make Way for the Ducklings* in Boston, or camping and nature books, you'll find something pertinent to your travels available for every age child. Check out your local children's bookstore or library.

For children ages 8 and up, look for the *Kidding Around* travel book series from John Muir Publications (800-285-4078) for books covering the history and sights to see for New York City, Boston, Chicago, Philadelphia, Washington, DC, San Francisco, San Diego, Los Angeles, Atlanta, Sante Fe, Hawaii, Seattle, and the National Parks of the Southwest. (Plus Paris, London and Spain!)

Travel Games (No equipment required!)

There are many favorite games which require no equipment and are perfect for passing the time in many situations but they don't work for children under the ages of 2 or 3. For the very young, hand games, music, identifying objects by color and rotating toys work best. Once children are old enough you can engage in:

• **Twenty Questions**—write down the name of a person, place or thing. Everyone tries to guess the name by asking a total of 20 questions that can only be answered by "yes or no."

• **Ghost**—a spelling game where you try NOT to spell a word. The first person thinks of a word and says the first letter. Each person then adds a letter and the person completing a word (must be more than 3 letters) loses. The loser is assigned first a G, then an H, until the person who loses five times becomes a GHOST and the game begins again.

• **Geography**—can be played simply (by naming all

states) or in a more complicated manner (by naming them alphabetically). Other variations include naming state capitals, naming border states, or spelling state names backwards. Also you may name a location and the next person must name a geographical location that begins with the final letter of the location just given, and so on.

• **"I'm Going on a Trip and I'm Packing ..."**—a memory game where each person repeats the first sentence including the previous item mentioned, and then adds one of their own. This continues until someone forgets an item in the sequence.

• **Alphabet Game**—everyone competes to find all letters of the alphabet, one at a time, in sequence, from signs, license plates, and billboards. You can use menus in a restaurant.

• **Reverse**—spell words backwards for others to guess.

• **Buzz**—in this round-robin counting game, the number 7 (or a number of your choice) must be avoided. A person must say "buzz" when a number with a 7 in it comes up.

• **"I Spy..."**—a guessing game where the leader suggests something seen in a certain color ("I spy something red") or size ("I spy something smaller than a backpack") that the others have to guess what the something is.

• **Make Believe**—is just that! Ask each other questions such as, "If you had wings, where would you fly?" or "What animal would you like to be?"

• **Good Luck/Bad Luck**—take turns making up sentences such as, "What good luck we found the party place!/ what bad luck the party was yesterday!" Or one person makes up the "good luck" part and the next person must come up with the "bad luck" ending.

The Modern Technology of Tapes

Surely nothing has changed travel entertainment more than children's audiotapes, regardless of the child's age. Be they music or stories, from birth to budding teen, tape recorders are the best!

• Take children's tapes to play in the car's tape deck or a child's cassette player. Raffi, Sesame Street, *Wee Sing* song cassettes tapes are just a few of many available.

• Buy picture books accompanied by tapes. Or tape stories yourself before you leave, or check out others from the library. You can record a story as you read it in the car and your child can play it back and read along with the book. Or have Grandma/Grandpa read some books or record stories on tape to bring.

• In addition to tapes and book-tape sets you can find in stores or libraries, you might wish to get the catalog, *Music for Little People,* PO Box 1720, Lansdale, CA 90260, (800) 727-2233 for more options.

• Include blank tapes to record some of your travel experiences, car songs or silly stories.

• Have older children interview kids and fellow travelers on planes, at historic sites, etc. Let them record their impressions of museums or describe the Grand Canyon on tape.

• By all means, bring players with individual headsets.

• And bring along extra batteries!

Keep in mind, you don't have to depend on tapes to enjoy the fun and entertainment of singing. If you're at a loss for words, you may want this handy helper for the words to 30 favorite songs: the 32 page, 3" x 5", *Sing Along Songs for Kids* is perfect. Send $1 and a long self-addressed, stamped envelope (2 stamps, please) to Practical Parenting, Dept TRL-Songs, Deephaven, MN 55391. (See page 138.)

Souvenirs

Acquiring souvenirs can be a high point of the trip. Just decide on some criteria for spending money on them. Discuss beforehand what kids can and cannot buy. Establish limits and stick to them. Allocate travel money for their items but encourage them to enhance their buying power with some of their own money.

Many families decide on one item of interest that will serve as an addition to their collection of Christmas tree ornaments so trip memories are reestablished each December. Others must commemorate each place with the appropriate T-shirt. Many like to collect one nice item unique to the region.

If you're going to the beach you'll be bringing back shells. Favored rocks can—and will—be found everywhere! (Be prepared by bringing collection containers.)

Remember to plan space in returning luggage for those vital memory-makers which are sometimes larger than planned.

Postcards are good for kids who don't have cameras. They can also be collected in self-stick photo albums or in a heavy duty self-closing plastic bag. A few large manila envelopes can also hold a collection.

Souvenirs keep kids entertained en route. They can be discussed, cataloged, admired, arranged and played with while traveling. Once home, their value for show-and-tell or sharing with friends and family often outweighs their actual cost.

We have three girls. Coming up with affordable souvenirs for our week in California took some thought. One collected the brochures for places we visited, another collected an imprinted napkin from wherever we were, and the last one got to pick a postcard from each place we visited.

Donna Johnson, Windom, MN

Chapter Four

SLEEPING AWAY FROM HOME

Sleeping away from home is easiest with a new baby. We may hesitate to travel with an infant because of the newness of the situation and all the upheaval already caused by the baby. But babies can and do sleep anywhere.

After your baby is 6 months old, it will be harder to sleep "just anywhere," due to his or her growing mobility and the fact that travel now will probably begin to affect sleep patterns. After 1 year of age, your child will be familiar enough with his or her own bedroom to be aware of and stimulated by different surroundings. If you've sheltered your child from changes in environment and schedules, travel may be more disruptive.

It's a good idea to get your baby used to sleeping and eating in different places as early as possible, so all the adjusting won't have to be done during the trip. Before you leave, have your child try sleeping in different rooms in the house or apartment. Make a game of it for a toddler.

Mentally program yourself to accept a child who won't take a nap or go to bed at the usual time. Let your child sleep when tired, and try to forget your usual schedule. Accept whatever comes as your new routine and you will be much more at ease. When home, you can get back to your routine.

Settling In

What, for you, is a routine trip may be for your child an exciting adventure that can't be missed, even for sleep. Since a good night's sleep can help ensure the success of the following day, do everything you can to make your child feel comfortable and secure at night. Extra reassurance from you can help.

One way to do this is to settle in to where you'll be staying the night *prior* to having dinner.

Unfortunately, an overtired child does not necessarily go to sleep faster or stay asleep or sleep longer despite the logic of the situation.

What Is a Bed?

If you haven't brought your own portable crib or small playpen along, you can arrange for a crib to be set up in a hotel/motel room before you arrive so a sleeping baby can be put right to bed. If the baby is awake, the crib provides a place to put him or her safely while you unload and unpack. If the place at which you'll be staying doesn't supply a crib and you'll be there for any length of time, arrange to rent a crib from a rental agency. There are a variety of small, collapsible beds (and even some inflatable ones) in stores or listed in mail-order catalogues.

But a bed (defined only as where your baby will sleep) can be improvised easily and eliminates the need for extra items to carry.

• Make a bed for an infant in a padded drawer or laundry basket placed on the floor. A pillow with a towel wrapped securely around it makes a good pad.

• Make a '"nest" for an infant, but only one who can't turn over yet, on an unused big bed by surrounding the infant with pillows and extra blankets rolled up (and, of course, with a waterproof pad underneath).

• Or place a small inflatable wading pool on top of a bed. Line it with a soft towel or blanket.

43

• Make a low hammock for a baby by tucking the ends of a sheet between the mattresses of two beds spaced about three feet apart. Place a pillow or cushion on the floor under the sheet to make it more comfortable. Baby rests on the cushioned floor, and the hammock sides keep away drafts.

Other Improvisations

• Let your child sleep with you in your bed if you are used to the "family bed" system. Or let your child fall asleep in the family bed, then move the child after he or she is asleep.

• If you have more than one child, position them sideways on a queen- or king-size bed. That will increase their "sprawl" space.

• Push the bed your child will use against a wall and place chairs against the remaining sides to prevent roll-offs.

• Bring along a bedrail that secures between the mattress and the box spring, to provide extra security for a toddler unaccustomed to sleeping in a strange bed. Some vacation spots will provide bedrails.

Getting Children to Sleep in Hotels/Motels

Whatever your sleeping arrangements, be prepared to take extra time to get your child to sleep. Sometimes it's necessary to turn off the light and wait outside in the hall until a child settles down. Once your child is asleep, you and your spouse can take turns going for a swim, a cup of coffee or a stroll. Or make your own private time in the room together by watching TV softly or playing an adult game you've brought along for just these moments. Often the TV (or radio) will lull your child to sleep.

• Help a baby fall asleep by putting the crib against the window (a well-secured one) and closing the drapes around the outside of the crib. When you go to bed, put the drapes back so the morning light doesn't wake the baby.

   • Camp out in the bathroom after your child is securely in bed and until he or she is asleep.

Making Your Room Comfortable and Safe

   • Consider bringing along your own crib bedding. Most places provide too-large linens that won't "stay put." Your own baby blanket will also be especially useful here.

   • Use a spread or an extra blanket from a bed to improvise a bumper pad for a crib if one is not supplied.

   • Ask for extra towels. With kids along you will inevitably need some more.

   • Check the safety features in your room if you have a busy toddler: electrical outlets, loose or dangling cords, windows (if there are no screens, keep windows locked or open from the top), lamps that can be pulled over—everything you've already checked and corrected at home.

   • Remember, you can move and rearrange furniture to suit your needs. Just return it back to its original position before checking out.

   • Keep your room as tidy as you can for both comfort and efficiency in getting up and on your way to a day's travel or fun. If you'll be in the hotel for more than a couple of nights, unpack clothing and store suitcases in the closet.

   • Use a clean wastebasket for a toy chest if clothing takes up all the drawer space.

Listening In

Room intercoms are wonderful items for parents who travel. They are good for:
- Visiting at a relative's house when the baby is sleeping in a distant room.
- Keeping tabs on older kids if you can't get adjoining rooms in a hotel/motel (and even then).
- Allowing you to be outside while your baby is sleeping without the need to keep checking.
- Knowing if another child is "checking" the baby inappropriately
- Having at home to check on your sleeping baby.

Intercoms come in two parts. The transmitter is placed near the sleeping baby, and the receiver is placed wherever it's convenient for you. Each part plugs in or uses batteries. Another type uses your own radio as the receiver.

Receiving-only intercoms cost from $25 to $35. Two-way intercoms cost between $40 and $60. Check with a local electronics store.

Visiting Friends and Relatives

Staying with people you know can be the greatest and simplest vacation or visit, or the most difficult and trickiest; it depends on how adaptable both families are and probably on your host family's experience with children.

Remember that if there isn't an infant or toddler in the house you're visiting, you'll be responsible for whatever childproofing measures are necessary for your own children's safety. Some grandparents will be comfortable childproofing their homes; some don't feel it fits for them. Don't take lack of interest in childproofing as an insult. You too may feel differently about infants in your home twenty years from now.

Each gift-giving holiday we give Grandma and Grandpa a toy of the kids' choice for them to keep at their house, thus building an entertainment supply for visits. Grandpa was especially pleased last Christmas when he received a Cookie Monster target game with Velcro balls!

Vickie Ploucher, Kalamazoo, MI

Making Yourselves Welcome

• Take a baby blanket to make a spot for play or napping.

• Ask for an old, large bath towel or a sheet of plastic or newspaper to put under a high chair—especially if you are eating in a carpeted room.

• Bring along a waterproof sheet (or flannel-backed pad or tablecloth) to protect surfaces when changing your baby, and also to protect mattresses. An old shower curtain will do, too.

• Protect a tablecloth by putting a plastic place mat under your child's setting.

• Plan some family time together away from your hosts to give them a break and some privacy.

• Clean up your own messes!

For a Place You Visit Regularly or for an Extended Period

• Leave an extra bottle, nipple, pacifier, or any other items that are inexpensive enough to duplicate and don't take up a lot of room. (Even keep an emergency "kit" in the car.)

• Buy a used portable crib or a gently used crib, possibly from a store that specializes in children's used furniture. Repaint it (with unleaded, nontoxic paint) for a new look.

• Rent a portable crib in advance from a rental company at your destination. Rental companies often are near airports. Or ask your hosts to arrange this, and reimburse them when you arrive.

• Arrange in advance for a weekly diaper service. Have the first set of diapers delivered before you arrive.

• Arrange to borrow or rent a car restraint if you'll be arriving by plane and you don't want to carry your own. Be sure that it is at the airport when you're being picked up. Or rent a car from a major company, as they often will provide car seats.

Safety at Grandma's

Do ask your parents to childproof for your impending arrival but don't be perturbed if they don't. It's been a long time since they've been around little ones and perhaps they themselves didn't really believe in childproofing. They may not have done it "back when" but they probably didn't own as much "stuff" then either. So bring outlet covers, doorknob covers, etc. as needed. A few bungee cords (or even pipe cleaners) can be used to secure kitchen or bathroom cabinet doors and a small hand towel thrown over the top of a bathroom door can prevent a small child from locking him- or herself in.

• Check the tops of dressers for medications, sharp pins or items that could be interesting enough to a small child to cause him or her to swallow it.

• Check that any grandparent medications are safely locked up and/or have childproof caps, including medications in handbags.

• Remember to bring your bottle of syrup of ipecac with your own travel items—*just in case!*

Chapter Five

EATING OUT
AND EN ROUTE

It's important to be flexible about when you eat. Missed meals can be compensated for by several healthy snacks, even if this doesn't fit your notion of what a meal should be. As reassuring as schedules are, sometimes they need to be disregarded. Close attention to your child's signals of hunger and boredom is the key to keeping your mobile family comfortable.

If it's at all possible, take a bottle, snack, or mini-meal with you wherever you go. That way you can offer the favored and familiar—important to a good trip for a baby or toddler. Even if your toddler eats table foods, it's wise to have a jar or two of his or her favorite prepared baby food at the bottom of your bag. These don't have to be refrigerated, and they are good insurance.

**Children behave best when their stomachs
are full and their bladders are empty.**

Feeding the Baby

Since formula or breast milk is all your infant needs for the first four to six months, your limited menu selection simplifies travel needs.

49

If you are thinking about weaning your baby from the breast or the bottle in preparation for the trip, think again. Nursing or bottle feeding will provide continuity for your child, and a major change such as weaning during your trip could have the reverse effect from what you had wished.

Nursing Etiquette

Fortunately today it is no longer necessary to banish yourself to a hidden corner if you're nursing.

• Learn how to nurse your baby in your front-pack carrier. Practice at home.

• Drape a light blanket or cloth diaper over your shoulder and over the baby's head while nursing. An attractive shawl or poncho also works well.

• Cover yourself with a large towel or terry robe when you're at the beach.

• Look in maternity stores for special tops with concealed openings for nursing mothers.

• Wear blouses, sweaters, or T-shirts that can be lifted at the waist—they're more discreet than tops that button down the center. If you wear a button-down top, unbutton from the bottom for the same effect.

• Try wearing a normal stretch bra for nursing. It's easier to lift one than to unhook a nursing bra.

• Remember patterned tops hide leaks better than solids.

• Don't nurse your baby while the car is moving unless you absolutely must, and if you must, it's safer to nurse in the back seat. It is possible to nurse while both mother and baby are restrained. With your baby in a rear-facing car restraint, you can lean forward toward your baby while still using your own shoulder harness.

• Be sensitive to the fact that there will be people who will be uncomfortable if you nurse in a public place and don't feel you must if you are uncomfortable nursing there.

Bottles and Solids

• Treat yourself to some bottled, ready-to serve formula that doesn't need refrigeration. It's more expensive but very convenient. Take sterilized water in the same size bottles for a thirsty (not hungry) baby.

• Carry plastic (not glass) baby bottles to avoid the mess and danger of a broken bottle.

• Put liquid or powdered formula into your bottles or disposable plastic bags in advance and close securely until needed. (Use four scoops of powdered formula to eight ounces of water, or follow instructions on the container.)

• Carry dry milk for a bottle-fed toddler who no longer uses formula. Put ⅓ cup (or 2 ⅔ ounces) in the bottle and add water to make 8 ounces when you're ready to feed the baby.

• Consider buying bottle "straws" that fit into bottle nipples even before your baby can sit upright alone or hold his or her own bottle. These "straws" allow a baby to hold a bottle without tilting the head back and gulping in troublesome air bubbles.

• Bring a wide-mouth thermos filled with hot water— great for warming up a bottle and helpful for cleanups.

• Toss some ice cubes in the milk/formula bottle to keep it cold longer.

• Get your little one used to room temperature or cold bottles and you'll save yourself a lot of preparation time while in transit.

• Pack instant baby cereal, premixed with powdered formula or dry milk, in separate, resealable plastic bags. When you stop to eat, pull out one of the packets, add warm water and serve.

• Keep the baby's food at just the right temperature on a short trip by storing the food in an insulated six-pack bag. Or heat small (4-ounce) unopened jars of baby food and place them inside a 10-ounce wide-mouth thermos.

• Pack the baby's long-handled feeding spoon in a plastic toothbrush case and keep it handy in your purse or diaper bag. Bring an extra spoon in case you lose one. Or just tape a small baby spoon or a disposable plastic one to a jar of baby food.

• Consider mixing some pureed foods or baby cereal with your bottle of formula or milk to make an easy-to-serve meal.

• Never save strained foods or milk to serve as leftovers. Bacteria thrives in warm or room-temperature food.

• Bring along your baby food grinder so your baby can share appropriate food from your plate at a restaurant or at someone else's house.

My daughter has been boating and fishing with us since she was 3 weeks old. I take only necessities and improvise with what is available—a can of Similac can warm in the sun, and so can jars of food. She loves it!

Ann Kooperman, Turnersville, NJ

Eating on the Go

Bringing food from home and restocking along the way, if your trip is long, can be solutions to the problem of meals and eating on the go.

You save money and you can have more control over the family's diet by bringing along a well-stocked cooler. Commercial freezer packs are a good dripless investment, or pack ice cubes in heavy-duty freezer bags which keep melting cubes from leaking. A good insulated food carrier small enough to fit beneath the seat will be helpful.

Many gas stations or convenience stores have ice cubes when you need them. You'll also find them in motel and hotels.

Traveling and snacking go hand in hand, so don't be too concerned about diet. Basic easy sandwich fixings are still peanut butter, cheese/cheese spreads and luncheon meats.

Picnics whenever possible will keep your car cleaner and you won't have to worry about restaurant manners!

Food, Food!

As one experienced mother once said, a child cannot eat and whine at the same time.

• Tie a bagel to the car seat with a string for a toddler. It's better than an all-day sucker.

• Bring along a can of "squirt" cheese to serve on crackers Remove some of the stack of crackers from the box and the can will fit inside.

• Serve a container of yogurt with a straw inserted through the top lid for a spill-proof snack or meal.

• Bring a six-pack cardboard carton to hold napkins, juice cans, granola bars, etc.

• Use a shoe box lined with foil for a meal-in-a-box plate.

• Cut down on potty stops by avoiding salty foods that make youngsters drink more.

• Pack disposable items such as paper plates, cups, forks, spoons, and wipes. Remember—the trick to easy traveling is to cut down on your cleanup time.

Unfortunately, the things that make them the happiest are gum and food—the messier, the better. By the end of the week, the back seat and floor of the car could easily feed a family of five. If no one's screaming or fighting, who cares?
Cynthia Carlton, Los Angeles, CA

• Eat lunches and snacks at rest stops when you can, so everyone can get out of the car and get some fresh air and exercise.

• Pack snacks individually in small resealable plastic bags to make handing out food faster and easier.

I always bring the plainest, cleanest and most unappealing food possible, such as a bag of apples.
Dorothy Skelly, Minnetonka, MN

Beware of foods that might cause a child to choke or gag. An adult sitting in the back seat with a child who is eating is a good safety precaution. Remember that ice cubes and small, hard foods should be avoided for small children. Choking can be impossible to deal with while the car is in motion.

Safe Toddler Snacks

- cheese slices or chunks; string cheese
- bananas
- seedless grapes (cut in half for babies und
- other fruit (cut-up) such as orange slices or canned mandarin oranges.
- crackers
- bagels or frozen bagel sticks
- pretzels (preferably unsalted)
- dry cereal such as Cherrios
- small, cut-up sandwiches

Satisfying Thirst

To cut down on pit stops, take water rather than more *i*nteresting drinks. Kids will drink water only when they're really thirsty, rather than just because they like its taste.

- Make an X-shaped slit in a baby bottle nipple. When your toddler gets thirsty, invert the nipple inside the bottle and put a straw through the slit for a spill-proof (well, almost) container.

- Try boxed drinks with straws for toddlers—they love them. Although they're not entirely spill-proof, they are usually neat (though you may need to invest in the "non-squeezable" plastic holders for them) and they're disposable. Be careful when inserting the straw NOT to squeeze the box. These also freeze well and can be used to keep other food cool while they defrost en route.

- Bring along a trainer cup if you child uses one.

- Take collapsible drinking cups to use in the car and at drinking fountains that small children can't reach.

Try the small, narrow Tupperware cups that have sealable non-spill covers and fit into a small child's hand.

• Look for the children's thermos bottles with special spouts for a straw.

• Carry a biker's drinking bottle or the popular plastic squeeze drinking bottles (complete with an attached straw).

**Watch a child using a drinking straw in a car.
The straw could cause injury in case of a quick stop.**

• Refill an empty plastic soda bottle with water or take along your camping canteen. Both are good for trips.

• Fill a plastic jug half or three-quarters full with water. Freeze it. When you're ready to go, fill the jug to the top with tap water. The water will remain cold, and as the ice melts you will have additional cold water to drink. The jug can also double as an ice pack for your cooler.

• Never bring a drink that will stain if you spill it...*you will and it will!*

We hang our two children's Yogi Bear canteens from the garment hooks on each side of the back seat, filled with each one's favorite drink. When it's gone, they get no more, so they learn to sip.
                                Mrs. J. Putnam, Claremont, NH

I put a drink in one of those empty plastic lemon/lime dispensers so my daughter can just squeeze it in her mouth and replace the cap when she's finished. No spills—no mess! And she loves it.
                                B. Lipman, S.Windham, ME

Dealing with Drips and Spills

• Use absorbent cloth diapers for mopping up spills. Or keep a damp sponge in a plastic bag.

• Keep an extra change of clothes handy for accidents.

• Cut slits in the middle of some small paper plates or paper coffee filters. When it's time for treats such as Popsicles® or ice-cream bars, insert the sticks into the slits and let it catch the drips (well, at least some of them!).

• Cover the back seat of a car under your child with a beach towel to catch crumbs or put a piece of heavy plastic under the baby's car seat. You can often buy plastic car seat protectors from mail order catalogs, or consider the heavy-duty rubber "Seat Neat," which can be ordered from Prince Lionheart, Santa Maria, CA at (800) 544-1132.

• Bring bibs for feeding your baby on the go. A small terrycloth towel or cloth diaper, secured with diaper pins or spring clothespins, works well. Bibs can limit dirty laundry caused by constant drool.

Eating in Restaurants

Finding good places to eat with little ones can be difficult in a strange town. If you know someone who's been where you're going, ask for recommendations. Hotel and motel personnel often are good sources of information, too. Don't forget the Yellow Pages. Call and ask about the suitability of dining with children. Ethnic, family style and buffet restaurants usually are good choices. If you're trying to save money, make breakfast the biggest meal of the day—it's almost always less expensive than lunch or dinner.

Fast-food places which may offer outdoor playgrounds and picnic tables, if not the best in well-rounded nutritional selections (which you can supplement, anyway) have, in addition to their convenience, clean and fairly spacious rest rooms. Consider choosing a drive-in restaurant if you are traveling with a very fussy baby, or at least pick a noisy restaurant, where you won't be that noticeable!

You can ask any restaurant to fill your thermos with boiling water so that you can mix cereal, soup, or just heat up formula along the way or for breakfast the next day. Many will also restock your water jug with ice cubes.

You can also feed your baby first and then take your satisfied child with you while you enjoy your meal out. Save good adult restaurants for times when you can leave the children with a sitter.

It's wise to call ahead and make dinner reservations if you can and to check on the availability of high chairs, booster seats, and children's menus. Try to keep your meal schedule as close as possible to the one you follow at home, but eat early, rather than late, both to avoid the crowds and to keep the children happy you might want to dress your children in their pajamas at your dinner stop when you're traveling by car. This allows you to have them ready for bed when you arrive so they can be tucked in with minimum fuss.

The Young and the Restless

• Be sensitive and flexible about suitable placement of an infant seat. It will take up a lot of room on a restaurant table and can be in the way on the floor. A booth can be a good choice as a place for eating with a child in an infant seat. The seat can fit on the table or the seat.

• Eat out late if you have a baby who can sleep through the activity. Let the baby sleep in a carrier or on a pile of coats on the floor beneath the table.

• Let a baby play with an ice cube on the high chair tray. It's good fun as it melts. Don't give your baby a metal spoon or fork to bang on a tray. It does nothing for other diners' digestion!

• Do go outside with a crying child until calm is restored.

• Clear the table of condiments, candles, and other attractive nuisances within the reach of a bored child.

• Wait for the food to arrive before putting a baby in a high chair, but don't let a walking child circulate. It's dangerous, and it's annoying to other diners.

• Let your toddler sit in a seat facing a window. Cars and people will provide distraction. If you can't get a window seat, at least sit by a wall, to be out of the way.

• Keep a booster seat in your car to use in an unaccommodating restaurant. You can make a homemade seat from old catalogues wrapped in contact paper. Or your car restraint can act as a booster seat in a booth.

• Remember, backpacks with stand-up frames, a stroller, or even tying a toddler into a booster seat with a dishtowel can provide the child's seat you need.

• Avoid booth seats with an unrestrained toddler. (If you don't understand the wisdom of this tip, you will after you sit in a booth with a toddler.)

Portable High Chairs

Hanging high chairs, which attach to most tables, can be wonderful for travelers with small children. They are compact and can usually accommodate children up to forty pounds. Leverage makes these chairs work, but safe use depends on how and where you use it. Avoid using on a pedestal-style, glass top, card table or one with a table cloth or placemats.

Check for the table's stability before attaching the chair. In addition, check to see that your child's feet cannot reach anything nearby, so he or she can't "push off," especially possible with a picnic table over a bench or a booth table in a restaurant. Chairs with locks or clamps to hold them in place are best.

For traveling (or even for home use), you may prefer a fabric high chair that slips over the back of a chair or through backseat slats. (Obviously, they can only be used on certain types of chairs.) The fabric ties around the baby's bottom like a sling and ties at the back of a chair. If you sew, look for a pattern in a fabric store.

• Carry your own "restaurant kit," which might include children's utensils, towelettes, a high chair strap or belt, large bibs, a few small toys, crayons for drawing on the back of paper place mats or napkins, and even a few crackers. (Ask for a pot of warm water and an extra napkin to clean the table or high chair tray, if necessary. Or use a moist towelette.)

• Flip a coin to determine which adult will order the meal while the other takes an impatient toddler for a walk until the food arrives.

• If a tantrum occurs and can't be contained, an adult should take the child out while the other waits to have the food put in doggie bags or other containers. Later, enjoy a picnic in the hotel room.

Staving off Hunger

• If you can, order your meal by phone in advance.

• Ask the waiter which dishes take the least amount of "waiting" time.

• Let it be known that the children's meals can—and should—be brought first. Soup is usually a good and fast start.

• In addition to hot dogs and hamburgers, order grilled cheese sandwiches, scrambled eggs, Jell-O or ice cream for surefire winners.

• Carry a compartmentalized pillbox (available at drugstores) filled with cereal, raisins, or other small treats. Opening and closing the compartment "doors" will keep your toddler happy for quite a while.

• Ask for crackers, bread, or a bowl of white rice to be brought to your table before the main part of the meal, to satisfy a hungry child.

• Order an appetizer your child can share with you. A chef's salad or fruit platter can be shared, too.

• Bring most or parts of your child's meal with you into the restaurant. Wrap items separately (in aluminum foil, for instance) and let your child open the "presents."

• Ask the restaurant to split an order in the kitchen for a child who is not receptive to eating from the extra plate brought for meal sharing.
• Order a meal with doggie bag potential for a child who is suddenly no longer hungry but will be—once you've left!

• Let's hear it for salad bars!

> *rely ordered a meal when eating out with our*
> *their eyes were always bigger than their*
> *Believe me, I tried to negotiate a better*
> *with them beforehand—to no avail. I'd have*
> *...enty to eat just finishing what was left on their plates.*
> Bob Stahl, Golden Valley, MN

Passing the Time

• Practice counting! Count anything...chairs, customers, waiters, lights, and so on.

• Bring crayons (even when provided, they are seldom in good shape) or markers for drawing on paper napkins and paper placemats. Or keep small note pads on hand.

• Have a contest to guess how long it will take the waiter/ waitress to serve your food. Whoever guesses closest to the actual time the food arrives is the winner.

• Play *Hot/Cold*. One person thinks of a visible object while the other person(s) tries to guess what it is. You can only indicate Hot or Warm, if the guessing is close to the object, and Cold if you're far from it until it is correctly guessed.

• *Dot-to-Dot* and *Tic-Tac-Toe* played with any available paper has helped many a family successfully wait for their meal.

• In some appropriate places, a single small toy car can provide a good deal of entertainment on a smooth table.

• Take a trip to the bathroom for a pre-meal clean up or let one parent wait for the food while the other takes the kids for a short walk.

Keeping Cleanup Under Control

• Spread a piece of newspaper or plastic under the high chair of a child you know will drop and spill food.

• Bring your child's own training cup to avoid spills. A child can also "drink" from a baby bottle with the cap and nipple removed.

• Clean up table messes the children make, and point out any floor spills to a restaurant employee so they can be mopped up promptly.

• Tip helpful restaurant personnel generously!

Eating Where You Stay

Families traveling today make things easier for themselves by packing food from home to carry with them, buying it where they stay, or bringing in fast-food or already prepared meals to their rooms. Everybody enjoys the adventure of it all, and the savings in money can be considerable. Having food on hand can be particularly crucial when your toddler wakes up hungry at 6:00 AM.

• Have breakfast in your room. You can prepare a hot meal by mixing instant baby cereal with the hottest water from the tap. Provide individual boxes of cold cereal for older tots. The boxes are made to be used as bowls, but put back-up paper plates under them just in case. The assortment varieties can make fun vacation fare.

• Make ahead individual resealable plastic bags of cold cereal and a spoonful of powdered milk. All you do is provide water and a spoon and you have a quick breakfast. But wait until your child is old enough to be agile with this type of unsupported "cereal bowl."

• Keep small cans or boxes of juice, crackers, bread, peanut butter and fresh fruit in your room for quick snacks. Chill juice containers in the ice bucket provided, or bring your own small cooler. Or fill a sink with ice and cover it with towels. Even milk will stay fresh if you keep the ice supply constant.

• Visit a local market or roadside stand and buy fruits or vegetables that can be washed or peeled in your room to supplement the meals you bring in.

• Consider using room service for breakfast or dinner. It may not be as expensive as you think, since you can order what you want, and the kids can share single meals. And the mobility it allows the children doesn't have a price tag.

• Let the children "picnic" in the bathtub—an adventure for them and an easy cleanup for you.

Chapter Six

GOING BY CAR

The family automobile, whether it's a compact car or a full size van, offers the most privacy and freedom for travel. It also has the advantage of being familiar territory for infants and toddlers who are used to being strapped snugly into a car seat and going places with Mom and Dad. Just be sure to have the car serviced thoroughly before leaving!

If you're a night owl, leave for a long trip about the time your child usually falls asleep, and drive through the night. If you're not, don't drive when you're tired. In fact it's a good idea to have a guaranteed lodging whenever you'll be arriving after dinner time.

It's often best to travel at night or early in the morning so children can sleep in the car, but don't let them snooze so much that they'll be restless and overly active when you're ready to sleep. Expect to make frequent stops along the way for potty breaks and stretching. In fact, add one-third more to your normal driving time when you're planning your trip. If you only fill your gas tank half-full, you'll have to stop sooner that way.

Don't forget to consider rush hour traffic when you'll be driving through major cities in the AM or PM. It's time you don't want to spend in a car with kids.

Plan to end your travel days early. Children find it much easier to go to sleep if they have the opportunity to become familiar with new surroundings. A walk before supper or a dip in the motel pool can set the stage for a calm evening.

Safety Means Car Seats

It is impossible to protect an infant or child by holding him or her on your lap in a car. If there is an accident and your child is unrestrained, your arms will offer no protection whatsoever. A car seat is an absolute necessity. It's purpose is to distribute the force of a crash over the child's entire body and to prevent the child from flying forward. In general, the safest position for a car seat is always in the middle of the back seat.

You should already have your car seat by the time you bring your baby home from the hospital. Improperly restrained babies and children are in jeopardy. Don't use money as an excuse not to have a restraint—the expense is not that great. Isn't your child's life worth the price of three tanks of gasoline or a car radio? If you really can't afford to buy one, take advantage of one of the many rental programs available or check with your doctor's office, hospital, or in your community to see about obtaining a safety seat on loan.

Do NOT buy a used car seat if: it was made before January 1, 1981; if it has been involved in a crash; or if it doesn't have a label or an instruction manual.

Calling for Help

If you have questions about used car seats, recalls or if you want to report a defect, call the AUTO SAFETY HOTLINE at (800)424-9393. (In DC, call 366-0123).

For special help to specific questions about how to use and install your specific car seat, you can call Safety BeltSafeUSA at (800)745-SAFE. In California call (310)673-2666.

Renting a car at your destination? Many major car rental companies now rent children's car seats with their rental cars, depending on the city. Most require a refundable deposit. The seats usually are available only for round-trip rentals. Advance reservations are necessary.

Baby Comfort and Safety

• Keep a small baby centered in the car seat by tucking small baby blankets or rolled-up diapers between the sides of the seat and the baby's head.

• Make a baby more comfortable by placing a folded blanket under his or her knees so they are slightly bent.

• Have one of two adults ride in the back seat with the baby as an occasional option.

• Adjust harnesses on car restraints as you change the baby's clothing to adjust to weather changes.

• Backseats in the summer can be hot because they receive less air conditioning than the front seat. Conversely, the backseat receives less heat in the winter and can be cold.

The most important thing to remember is to use an appropriate restraint every time your child rides in the car. Make it an unquestionable and inflexible rule. All states (and several Canadian provinces) now have laws requiring restraints for small children.

Safety Belt Song
(sung to the tune of "Jingle Bells")

Safety Belts, Safety Belts, Wear them all the way.
Every time you're in your car, Any night or day, oh
Safety Belts, Safety Belts, Put them 'round your lap,
Then before you start to ride, Everybody—SNAP!
National Safety Council

Toddler Tactics

• Set a good example. Always buckle yourself in after you've buckled your child.

• Be sure all fingers are safely out of the way before closing the car doors. Make a game of having all hands reach for the sky, or have your child give himself or herself a hug before you close the door.

• Don't enable a child to play with door locks by putting car seats too close to doors. Hardware and auto stores sell safety locks that fit over standard push-down car door locks.

• Have your child make sure that everyone in the car is buckled. A child will often respond to responsibility.

• Make it a rule that the engine isn't started until everyone is safely buckled in. This means adults, too. Use the line, "Do you want me to get arrested?"

• Buckle one of your child's favorite large stuffed animals or dolls in the car seat when your child climbs out of it. Better yet, let your child do it. Next ride you'll know where the buckles are and your child will have a toy to play with.

• Stay calm while you are traveling with your child who may fuss about being restrained. If you have to stop the car to soothe him or her, do so. But don't unbuckle the belt.

• Let the car come to a complete stop before you unfasten the children's restraints and adults' seat belts.

Four Kinds of Car Seat Restraints:

Infant seats: These are for infants from birth to about 9 months (or 20 pounds). They are used semi-reclined and are to be used only facing backward in a front (unless the front passenger side has an air bag) or the back seat.

Convertible car seats: These can be used as infant safety seats (facing backward) and can be turned around and put in an upright position when the child gets old enough to fit a toddler car seat. These will cover weight from birth to 40 pounds. Don't place it on a front seat where there's an airbag.

Auto booster seats: These elevate a child who has outgrown the standard seat but still isn't tall enough to see out the window. Children can graduate to a booster seat once they reach 40 pounds or when their ears reach the top of the child safety seat.

Shield booster seats: These are used when only a lap belt is available. Read instructions carefully to see what is required of each model. These seats can double as booster seats in restaurants and elsewhere—but lightweight, inexpensive booster seats should never be used as car boosters.

An excellent resource for families wishing to buy child safety seats is a brochure available from the American Academy of Pediatrics. It spells out how to choose and care for a car seat. It also lists specific brands, descriptions, and prices of car seats currently on the market. For a free sample copy of the *Family Shopping Guide to Car Seats*, send a self-addressed, stamped business-size envelope to: Family Shopping Guide, American Academy of Pediatrics, PO Box 927, Elk Grove Village, IL 60009-0927.

Common Safety Mistakes Parents Make

Parents:

• diligently read everything on childbirth, nutrition, and parenting, yet fail to protect their children by not using the restraints properly every time they are in a car. Often they fail to read the manufacturer of car seat installation instructions or the car owners manual.

• bundle an infant in a blanket, making it impossible to secure the shoulder harness properly. A blanket can be tucked around the baby after the belt is buckled.

• forget to secure the seat with the car lap belt. If the lap belt does not fit around or through the frame, try another position in the car or try another type of seat. Be sure you have followed instructions correctly if you have difficulties. Don't use one with an automatic seat belt system.

• neglect to use the shoulder harness, or use it incorrectly. This makes the restraint itself potentially hazardous to a child. Many harnesses are too loose (only two finger widths should fit between the harness and the child's body) or are not threaded through the correct slots.

• neglect to fasten the top anchor strap, when required. Often this is because of uncertainty about how to affix the anchor, or unwillingness to bolt the anchor to the car.

• don't insist that grandparents, baby-sitters, and other caretakers put children in car seats when they are driving.

• don't wear seat belts themselves. They set a bad example, and risk the possibility of turning their safely-buckled children into orphans.

Safety Also Means . . .

- checking under and behind your car before backing out of your driveway.
- never leaving keys in the ignition while your car is parked.
- feeling the seat and seat-belt buckle on a hot summer day to be sure they will not burn a child's sensitive skin. (A towel makes a good seat cover on a hot day.)
- keeping the dashboard and rear window ledge free of loose objects that could fly off and hit a child if you have to stop suddenly. Even a box of tissues can be a hazard.
- keeping at least one window slightly open to ensure against any danger of carbon monoxide poisoning.
- never leaving a baby or toddler alone in a car.
- confining your pet—a loose dog or cat can be a dangerous distraction.
- locking your car when you get out. Children can climb in, release hand brakes, lock themselves in, and do all kinds of damage.
- locking all doors while traveling.

Car Seat Blues

When your child is awake and behaving well in a car restraint, a little positive reinforcement can go a long way toward keeping the peace. Talk and play with your baby to make riding in a car fun. Frequent praise and attention can teach your child that travel in a car restraint is a positive experience. Decorate the seat and personalize it for your baby to make it special. If your baby is in a rear-facing car seat, tape a brightly-colored picture to the seat of the car for visual stimulation. Or attach a soft overhead mobile to the car seat. Do remember, though, that nothing keeps little older ones entertained for very long, so be sure to stop frequently on long trips to let them stretch and get some fresh air.

What if, in spite of all your good intentions and best efforts, your properly restrained baby begins to scream as you drive down the interstate? Or your toddler chooses this time to throw a full-scale tantrum? Ideally, you'd pull off the highway to save the driver from a dangerous distraction and to soothe the child, but it's not always possible to do that at the exact moment you'd like to. If you can't stop, try distracting the child:

• Turn up the radio, play a tape, or sing a loud song. Babies aren't particular about your choice of tunes. They just enjoy the sound of your voice.

• Rub the baby's chest gently and talk in soft, soothing tones.

• Try talking gently into the baby's palm, or put his or her hand on your throat. The vibration the baby feels from your vocal cords may have a soothing effect.

• Bring out a new toy or a snack.

Back Seat Bickering

Fighting and bickering is normal behavior for kids traveling by car. (*Read that sentence again*). It doesn't mean you're a bad parent or that you have bad kids. Hopefully, this knowledge will make the inevitable easier for you to accept. (Note, I said accept, not "like" or "get used to.")

• Tell children over the age of 2 or 3 that if things get out of hand, you will pull the car off the road and stay there until they behave. It is usually wonderfully effective!

• Or you might want to go as far as stopping your car at the side of the road and telling your children to get out and go at it when they're standing outside and that, once they're finished, you all can continue on. Usually this breaks the tension and you can continue on your way.

"No One Said It Would Be Easy"

If my children fuss when I strap them in, I tell them I'm doing it because I love them.

Doreen Newell, Simpsonville, SC

My 1 year old loves rock 'n' roll, so I turn on the car radio and she has a blast as long as she likes the song. Otherwise, to keep her happy, we stick to short drives.

Cynthia Gillian, Texas City, TX

We've tried everything! When all else fails, sing! Never once has our singing failed to calm our daughter. We do get hoarse on long trips, though!

Paul and Leissa Thigpen, Julian, CA

My boys fussed when they were infants, but I never gave in and took them out. I guess I was most influenced when a Mercedes rear-ended my VW Beetle when my oldest was 3 months old. He was hardly shaken up.

Kathy Hickok, Delray Beach, FL

Up until about the age of 2, my son Chris (now 3) would cry and/or scream whenever he was in his car seat. Nothing amused him! Long trips were out of the question. Short fifteen-minute jaunts were long enough! Now our misery has finally paid off. Chris climbs into his car seat happily and even reminds us to buckle up.

Linda Newberry, Jermyn, PA

• **Rotate your seats.** Rotating everyone's seat is a time-honored practice when you have more than one and will minimize some disputes—although not all of them! Actually car fights seem to bother kids far less than adults. The best seat in the car (or train or bus) is usually the one your child is not in. Actually, we all know window seats are usually favored. Figure

73

out a rotation system that works for you—a timer, a time schedule, by the day, odds/evens, whatever.

• Consult with your kids before hand about how they think car disputes should be handled. Write these down and take these notes with you to use as needed.

• Use reverse psychology! "No, I don't think we'll go to ____(*Disneyland, the water slide, etc.*) because I can't stand the back seat fights!" You may elicit, "Oh, we won't fight and if we do, you can____." Quick, make a list of the options they offer and your problem may be solved—or at least, minimized.

• Keep your sense of humor. Turn a complaint into a joke.

• Praise good car behavior or, better yet, reward it!

I use a technique called "Mad Bag/Glad Bag" to help our children monitor their behavior when traveling. Each is given a "Glad Bag" (a fabric pouch) with spending money in it (the amount and denominations, i.e. quarters or dollar bills, decided ahead). The parent owns the "Mad Bag". When a child misbehaves, you determine how much he or she must deduct from their Glad Bag. Used in moderation, this system can work well. *P.S.* Give the kids the opportunity to earn their money back for good behavior!
Carole T. Meyers, Berkeley, CA

One of the best ways to prevent discipline problems is to keep the children happily occupied. If you're prepared with toys and activities, the trip will be more pleasant for everyone. Start a series of silly rules, such as hands up to hold up a bridge when you go under one, or holding your breath when you go by a cemetery, or not talking when crossing a bridge. Silly word games, from making up crazy menus to calling things by their wrong names, can fill a car with laughter and fun.

Keeping Sunlight out of Your Child's Eyes

• Bring a soft toy along that's big enough to shield eyes and can't get lost under the seat.

• Pick up a suction-cupped car window shade to place on an appropriate window. It can also prevent seats from getting too hot.

• Use strips of Velcro above a back side window to attach a shade (fabric, blanket) as needed.

Short Car Trips

Once you leave home in a car, it becomes a trip, no matter how far you go—be it to the store, a restaurant, or the other side of town. If you're planning a longer car trip, it's a good idea to take your child on a lot of errands and such to help him or her get used to riding.

Be Prepared

• Keep an emergency disposable diaper in your glove compartment or trunk. Include other extras, such as bandages, that might come in handy.

• Add a pacifier to your key chain, in case your child has an emergency need for one.

• Store an extra set of diaper pins on your key chain to use when tape-tabs lose their stick or for attaching a napkin as an instant bib, or for any quick repairs.

• Carry a stretch belt in your purse to use as a "safety belt" for a toddler in a grocery cart, shopping center stroller, or restaurant high chair.

• Keep a treat hidden in your handbag or glove compartment to tide you over when needed. (If the treat is noticed before you leave, it will probably be consumed immediately upon departure).

• Invest in a used stroller to keep in the trunk for those times you didn't plan to get out of the car, but do. A second car seat is also a good secondhand purchase if you have two cars. Be sure the seat was made after January 1, 1981; if it was, it must conform to certain safety regulations.

Shopping Center Lost and Found "Insurance"

• Bring along a child's harness or wrist harness if your toddler is very active and tends to wander. The harness may look "bad" to purists, but it can be a real lifesaver. To modify its look, decorate with ribbon trim or embroidery.

• Dress two or more ambulatory youngsters in matching T-shirts so they will be easier to spot in a crowd. In the winter, red hats are helpful.

• Discuss with your children instructions on what to do if they get separated from you. Practice "what if..." scenarios while in transit to shopping centers, amusement parks and the like.

• Create a special family whistle that children will recognize if they become separated in a crowd, and practice using it at home.

• Point out police officers or guards to children so they will know whom to ask for help if they get lost. This can be especially useful abroad, where children aren't familiar with the different uniforms.

Shopping Center Trips

• Place your own infant seat in the shopping center's stroller for easy mobility.

• Shop early before stores get crowded so you don't get stuck standing in a long check-out line holding an infant who suddenly needs to be fed.

• Tie toys to strollers with short strings to avoid the "I throw, you pick up" game.

• Attach a helium balloon to a stroller to intrigue and occupy a child—for a while.

• Bring a large shopping bag to hold hats, mittens, and snowsuits. Attach it to the stroller handle with a chain of two or three safety pins.

• Or bring along your backpack to hold purchases so your hands will be free.

• Remember that many department stores have food departments where you can buy a slice of cheese or a piece of fruit to appease a cranky child.

Long Car Trips

Some children travel well; others simply don't. A set of parents I know traveled extensively with their first and second children. They left for a year in Israel when the second was only 3 months old. But they opted to stay put for three years when their third child turned out to be a very bad traveler.

Other parents decide that long trips are simply not worth the hassle and tell their families that if they wish to see the baby, their house is open to them. Mental health for babies and parents can be an important ingredient for keeping all family ties intact! It is fair to classify a three-hour trip to Grandma and Grandpa's as a long car trip, not a short one. Don't fool yourself into thinking that any one-day outing will be without stress.

Plan on stops at least every 2 or 3 hours. Such rest stops will slow you down but are a necessary change of pace. If you decide to travel into the night, schedule a last stop so the kids can brush their teeth and wash their faces (they might even want to change into their pajamas).

Remember that your travel objective is to get there safely and happily. If your objective is to get there fast, you might be foregoing *safely* and you will surely forego *happily*. Once you're at your destination, try to keep car travel to a minimum.

AAA

(American Automobile Association)

Membership entitles you to free maps, tour books, Triptik maps, route-planning assistance, travel agent services, American Express travelers cheques, and discounts on car rentals and other goods and services. They also sell a 144 page Travel Activity Book for kids ages 4 and up.

Packing The Car

• Pack cereal, formula, small jars of baby food, extra bottles, and cleanup gear in a sturdy box that can be reached easily while you're on the road and carried in when you stop for the night. You may also want to include a bottle warmer or baby-food grinder.

• Make tissues, disposable wipes, and paper towels standard equipment in your car.

• Store children's clothes or bulky cold weather items in a duffel bag which will fit into the car or trunk and can double as a pillow. Or get duffel bags for all, for the same reasons.

• Pack each person's items in a laundry basket if you have room for it in the car. At your destination use it for dirty clothes so that when you get home, the basket and its contents can go straight to the laundry room.

• Pack children's clothes in different-colored pillow cases for easy identification.

• Consider bringing a small pillow for each child. For older children large pillows are appreciated.

• Keep a blanket or two handy during the winter in case your child gets cold, or in case you have car trouble and have to wait for help in the cold.

Our 2-year-old loves to "pack" for long car rides. She has her own large plastic mesh shopping bag and fills it with her choice of toys and books.
Maureen Wilkins, Ketchum, ID

• Carry one large plastic garbage bag for each day you plan to be in the car. This doesn't guarantee that the car will stay clean, but it will be a big help for nightly cleanups. Extras come in handy for dirty laundry. (Remember, these can be dangerous and should not be used for play by small children.)

• Car vacuums that plug into a lighter can be worthwhile.

• Consider investing in (or renting) a rooftop carrier to allow the inside of the car to be less cramped.

• Don't try to take everything to Grandma's. For example, a folding umbrella stroller and a small folding playpen that can double as a crib should serve most of your needs without taking up all your trunk space.

• And do be sure to pack a spare car key with another person, or perhaps on the car in a magnet holder (not placed under the hood if you must open the hood from inside the car).

Motion Sickness

Car sickness used to be a common problem for small children, but parents aren't talking about it much anymore. Increased use of car seats and smoother-riding cars may be the reasons. Having a plastic ice cream pail with a cover is a good insurance item to have on hand. (And a small bag of kitty litter to sprinkle on accidents is good for after the fact. It absorbs moisture and odor.) Infants rarely get motion sickness. It seems to occur most commonly between the ages of 2 and 12.

If your child is bothered by car sickness, there are precautions you can take:

• Keep your child on a high-carbohydrate, low-fat diet for a few days before the trip. Go easy on liquids—especially milk and soft drinks—just before you leave.

• Plan to eat nothing for 3 hours before leaving, as there will then be less to upchuck. A small glass of cola without bubbles (let it set for a half-hour first) may act as an anti-vomiting remedy.

• Have the child sit in the front seat, if the car restraint will fit there, so he or she can look forward out the window.

• Direct your child's attention to things outside the car in the distance, rather than at the side of the road. Don't let the child do close work such as looking at books or coloring.

• Open a window to let in fresh air, and don't smoke.

• Believe it or not, static electricity can cause nausea. If it's a problem, attach a wire or small chain to the rear axle so that it just touches the road.

• Offer Dramamine (now available as a liquid), Marezine or Bonine Wafers as a preventative measure for children 2 years or older, but check with your doctor first. Administer at least 30 minutes to an hour before traveling. (Patches applied to the skin to prevent motion sickness for adults are not advised for young children.)

• If nausea is severe, stop the car and have the child recline with eyes closed and head motionless.

The number of potty stops and diaper changes will always be in direct proportion to the amount of liquid consumed in transit!

Rest Stops

If you treat stops as interesting experiences rather than delays, everyone will have a much better time. If you can get up and moving early in the morning, make breakfast your first stop. Make a game out of finding a good breakfast restaurant.

There's no need to stop at a scheduled time if everyone is happily occupied or napping, but about every two hours take a break so everyone can stretch and so mobile children can run and burn up some energy. The best rest stop is one that offers both a stretch and food—think picnic. If you haven't brought the fixin's with you, you can stop at a store and pick up everything you need. Many towns have centrally located park areas; ask about them. Or just stop when you see some picnic tables, and break out a special snack you've been saving.

• When you stop, park in the shade, or cover the children's car seats with blankets to prevent them from becoming "hot seats."

• Stop at a mall if the weather is bad. Some children can run off energy there.

• Let everyone know that you are planning to stop, so the kids will have something to look forward to and so older children will have time to put toys away and put on shoes. Wake a sleeping child at least 10 minutes before stopping so he or she can "regroup" rather than be grumpy at a rest stop.

• Play Frisbee, time a race against the minute hand of your

watch, do jumping jacks or play a game of tag—any activity to work off energy.

• Be sure toddlers use the bathroom before you leave so you don't have to stop five minutes later.

Entertainment Especially for Car Travel

• Make or buy a slipcover for the front seat with pockets that hang over the back to hold books, games, and toys. Or use a large cloth bag with a strap that fits over the head rest of the front seat.

• Tie small toys (preferably soft ones) to your child's car restraint so they won't get lost in the car and you won't have to hunt for them constantly.

• Stretch an elastic cord (with hooks on each end) between the hooks on each side of the back seat and tie soft toys within reach of the child's car seat.

• Keep some of the toys in the trunk, and stop occasionally to trade an old toy for an unfamiliar one.

• Pack a few toys in a small box that will fit between two children's car restraints in the back seat so both can reach them. Or fill a plastic dishpan to hold favorite toys and books.

• Include a toy telephone. They're wonderful for holding pretend conversations between cars.

• Try binoculars! They're good for keeping a child looking for license plates, reading bumper stickers, etc.

• For rest stops, remember toys such as inflatable beach balls, balloons, and, for older children, jump ropes.

It Worked for Us

We carefully plan routes that go by state parks when we take long trips. That way we have nice places to stop and eat and play with the girls. It's much nicer than feeding a baby on the side of the road with cars whizzing by. The scenery is nicer on back roads, too.

G. Moore, Houston, TX

At gas stops, everybody, including toddlers, gets out and exercises, and then changes places in the car (move that car seat, too, to give that sitter a different traveling partner and view). At the picnic stops, we've had our older ones do ten laps around the picnic tables!

Anita Holland, Minnetonka, MN

When my children were small, we always brought a large empty coffee can with a lid to use as a portable toilet or barf bag. (Yes, we used it!)

Sidney Milstone, Lathrup Village, MI

I point out trucks to my son and he talks nonstop about their color, size, contents, etc. I make sure his car seat is raised high enough so he has a clear view. My l-year-old is afraid of traveling at night, so I place his car seat beside me up front and open the glove compartment. It has a small light inside that serves as a night light for him.

Janet Stabile, Ellington, CT

My son hated being in the seat at night. We got him a small flashlight after I finally figured out that car and street lights were scaring him.

Michael Doesburg, Orange, CA

• Provide a hard surface for writing. Stash markers, coloring books, transparent tape, and other non-messy art supplies in an aluminum cake pan with a lid. The closed pan serves as a work surface. An old attache case can serve the same purpose. A cookie sheet works well too and both can be used as a table for making puzzles. For just a writing or drawing surface, use a clipboard.

Books, Lego, Etch-a-Sketch, and Colorform stickers for the car windows help keep my children occupied. Songs and frequent stops are important.
Becky Gammons, Beaverton, OR

• Make a lap tray for a child in a car seat. A folding bed tray probably won't fit, but you can make one from a sturdy box. If you're handy, make a wooden one with hinges for folding sides. Be sure to have raised edges to keep toys from rolling off.

• Bring an empty magnetic scrapbook for your toddler to fill with postcards, brochures, and other mementos of the trip. Keep you eye out for things to put in this memory book.

• Encourage older children to keep mileage charts to record the distance driven each day. Let them mark your route with a highlighter to track your trip.

• Log expenses in a travel journal. It invites discussion and interaction. An older child can act as bookkeeper.

• Play "*Mommy Says...*" (like Simon Says). Mommy (or Daddy) says, "*Touch your ear,*" or "*Point to the car roof,*" etc.

Bubbles! At any age kids like them. They're so small and transparent they don't block the driver's view. They're inexpensive, and if they spill, what happens is you have one clean spot on the seat or floor.

Sandi Mink, Detroit, MI

Auto Activities

• Keep a list of each different state seen on license plates. Some parents offer 25¢ a state and a dollar bonus if they find all fifty states.

• Guess the correct make of cars in your lane.

• Encourage kids to extend their arms above their heads to touch the car roof when going under a bridge to "hold it up".

• Look for *"pediddles"*—finding cars with only one head-light on (obviously a night game).

• Or "slug bug"—sighting Volkeswagen "beetles."

• Pick up a copy of Rand McNally's 80 page *Kid's U.S. Road Atlas* when traveling cross-country. There are easy-to-use maps for all 50 states plus games, mazes, puzzles and more. Your book store or children's learning store has books like this and other to keep your kids occupied. Stop there before leaving.

• Or look for a copy of Klutz Press's *Kids Travel: A Backseat Survival Kit* for ages 7-13. It's crammed full with puzzles, games and projects.

> *We have a "Navigator's Hat"—a painter's cap decorated with pins of the different places we visited. Each child takes turns becoming the navigator and wears the hat when reading the trip map.*
>
> Dorothy Jordon, New York, NY

• Be prepared. Be over-prepared! *Miles of Smiles: 101 Great Car Games and Activities* by Carole T. Meyers (Carousel Press)can be ordered by calling (510) 527-5849. Its 8"x 5" size fits into your glove compartment. Games are for preschoolers to junior high students. Even the book title is a game. (All players smile at the people in the cars next to them. The trick is to keep count of how many people you can get to smile back at you.)

Car Music To Entertain and Delight

If you don't wish to be the sole entertainment for your children, be prepared with audio tapes to get you through. Here's my favorite—one that I put together (*yes, I'm biased*) that is available three ways:

Sing Along Travel Songs

19 favorite classic kids' songs on 30 minutes of tape for ages 1 and up. Songs include: *Riding in the Car, Jack & Jill, Row Your Boat, Twinkle Twinkle, Kookaburra, Over the River, Sailing, Comin' Round Mountain, etc..*

• Cassette alone $8.95
• Cassette in album case with the words to the songs $9.95
• Deluxe: album case with a gift pack of Mrs. Grossman's travel stickers—5 designs! $12.95

Available from PRACTICAL PARENTING, Dept T-Audio, Deephaven, MN 55391. Add $2.75 for postage and handling. Call (800) 255-3379.

At Home On The Road

Motor homes, or more accurately, recreational vehicles, can be a wonderful way to travel as a family. They can be rented from agencies or private parties. It's not necessarily a cheaper way to travel but it's convenient and fun. There's room to move around; there is easy access to food and to toilet facilities; and it provides a comfortable "camping" adventure. You'll need to check out campground access and be prepared to pump out the waste reservoir holding tank. You'll also need to learn how to back up VERY carefully, but you'll definitely be "king of the road."

We parked our vehicle early in the day in the middle of the centrally-located parking lot of a water amusement park in Wisconsin Dells. It acted as our home base for a fun day. We could regroup, snack and begin again. We could keep tabs on our school-age children but could give them a good deal of independence.

Ros Nemer, Hopkins, MN

The Recreation Vehicle Industry Association, P.O. Box 2999, Reston, VA 22090 1-800-47-SUNNY is the national trade association that publishes a rental directory and a "How-to" booklet. Call for the current price.

• Or try Cross Country Motor Club at (800)225-1575; Cruise America at (800)327-7799 or Club Travel Motorhome Rentals at (800)234-Club.

• Or look for RV information on the Internet at http:// www.rvrent.com or at http://www.clubtravel.com.

Campsite Accommodations

Remember that although many campsites require reservations, most don't. Still if you want to be assured of a space call for reservations early in the season.

Campsite information is available from the National Park Service, P.O. Box 37127, Washington, DC 20013-7127. For reservations in selected national park sites call Mistix (800)365-2267. Ask for Family Campsite reservations brochure. The U.S. Forest Service has over 500 campgrounds nationwide. Reservations can be made by calling Mistix at (800)283-2267.

For a free state-by-state list of campgrounds and RV park associations call Go Camping America at (800)477-8669.

The Sierra Club offers hiking and backpacking trips for families with children ages 5 and up. Call (415)923-5630.

There are lots of good park guide books geared for traveling with children. Check your local bookstore and library.

And, of course there is the Internet. For a central 'library' for camping enthusiasts', campgrounds, RV suppliers, camping and travel information and more, visit web site: http://www.Kiz.com/campnet/html/campnet.htm.

Camping With Kids

Choose a campground with bathrooms, laundry facilities and a general store for your first outing. Pick a campsite convenient for children. For instance, you may wish to be as close as possible to the bathroom or showers. You may feel safer (and be safer) if your campsite is not near a road, lake or stream. As with any trip, accept each moment for its own enjoyment. Original plans and destinations sometimes have to be modified. Don't expect a child of any age to take a camping/hiking trip as seriously as you do. Even when preschoolers can hike a bit of a distance, you should not try to push the same distances two days in a row. And build up your stamina before you go if you'll be carrying your child in a backpack.

Getting in Gear
• Do a practice run in your backyard. On-site is not the

place to learn how to set up a tent. The same goes for using the cookstove and lantern.

• Protect your bag with a flannel-coated waterproof sheet if a baby is sleeping in your sleeping bag with you. (Good for newly-trained toddlers, too!)

• Use a regular-sized sleeping bag folded under to half-size for a toddler. The extra padding makes it more comfortable.

• Include rain gear, boots and jackets when packing, no matter what. Select clothes with an eye to layering. Have at least two complete sets of layered clothes per person.

• Pack some clothing and gear in plastic pails of various sizes that you can use for dishwashing, hand laundry and grooming. A large plastic container with a lid makes a great "mini" laundry tub for little items. Just add a little soap, put on the lid and shake. The shaking is more efficient than swishing in a pail.

• Arrive at your campsite midday, not late at night. Involve your kids, when they're old enough, in setting up camp.

• Bring a thin rug to put in front of the tent(s) to avoid tracking in dirt. Also, make it a rule to leave shoes outside.

• Bring a backpack for baby; a playpen and harness for a toddler. Some carry an umbrella to keep the sun off an infant in a backpack. A baby should, at the very least, have his or her head covered by a bonnet and skin protected with sunscreen.

• Use empty plastic bread bags for soiled diapers and wet items. Avoid the odors of damp, soiled clothing by packing fabric softener sheets in your laundry bags.

• Use a small inflatable wading pool for a child's bathtub. You can add a quilt or pad and use it as a crib or playpen.

• Bring collapsible lightweight chairs for everyone.

• Flashlights for safety and fun are a must. They can be used in a tent for hand-shadow games.

• Make up a nature box which might include books on birds, rocks and trees. Pack plenty of plastic bags, jars and boxes to hold collections. Give the kids collecting assignments.

• Bring empty plastic catsup or mustard containers to slip over tent stakes and prevent stubbed toes.

• Put mosquito repellent on the zipper and entrance seams to your tent.

Trail Tips

Have kids hike (if in a group) with non-family members. They complain less.

• Let the children plan the route.

• Praise your novice hikers frequently.

• Help children pace themselves. Distraction is one subtle technique and resting frequently is another. And, oh yes, walk at the pace set by the slowest family member.

Camp Food

Remember that children need to refuel more often than adults do.

• Don't forget graham crackers, marshmallows and chocolate bars to make s'mores at your evening campfire.

• To be sure you're prepared for anything, travel with food and drink in the car at all times (even if you plan to buy most supplies at your campground). When kids are outdoors, they tend to drink more than they usually do.

• Provide each child with a child-size backpack for water, snacks—and collecting treasures.

• One cooler is good, but two are better.

• Consider taking along your own drinking water, if you don't trust the water at the campground. Sometimes it's just the fact that water varies from region to region and can upset children's more sensitive systems. You don't want the kids to get diarrhea! Do NOT let the kids drink from a stream, lake or pond unless the water has first been purified with water purifying tablets.

If I've learned one thing in all my years in the rough, it's that kids remember the spectacular boners with more fondness than they do most nature lessons.

Kathleen Kunz, Norman, OK

Safety

• Store fishing gear, knives and matches up and away from children's reach in a sock pinned to a tree branch.

• Give preschool and school-age children whistle necklaces to blow in case of emergency.

• Teach kids to *"Hug A Tree"* and stay where they are if they suddenly find themselves alone. (Some put bells on toddlers.) Bright colored clothes are always a good idea.

• Watch toddlers carefully, especially when you are near a fire pit which is still hot. Never leave fires unsupervised.

• Teach children not to eat wild plants and berries.

• Pack a first-aid book and a good first-aid kit, tweezers for splinters, and take along some syrup of ipecac—*just in case*!

Chapter Seven

GOING BY AIRPLANE, TRAIN, OR BUS

If you don't travel by car, your destination, your budget, and your personal inclinations will help you choose among three alternatives: the airplane, the train, and the bus. Flying is the fastest, a real blessing for long-distance travel with babies or toddlers. Despite lack of space for babies and baggage, and possible (or should we say, probable) delays and discomfort from changes in cabin pressure, it's the easiest way to go.

Train travel offers the advantages of the passing scenery and a bit more freedom of movement, but it has its disadvantages, too. Riding the bus is probably your last choice—but it costs the least, and it will get you to corners of the country where planes and trains simply don't go.

Flying

The noise of a plane, even more than that of a car, helps lull a newborn infant to sleep. The more awake and aware toddler requires full-time entertainment from the parent. Obviously, the shorter the trip, the easier the job.

If you have a choice, make the time zones work with you rather than against you. North-south travel will always be less disruptive than east-west travel. But any trip causing more than a two-hour time adjustment will take just that—adjustment.

For a child prone to air sickness, avoid meals or hard to digest foods prior to take off. A seat in the front or the middle of the plane won't feel as much turbulence. And do carry easily available extra clothes for your child...and for yourself. Check with your doctor about using over-the-counter anti-nausea chewable tablets.

Take heart if all does not go smoothly. If your child travels regularly by air from infancy, by the time he or she is 3 or 4 years old the child will be a seasoned traveler who will be delighted with toilets that flush blue water and with overhead lights he or she can control.

Making Reservations

If you are pregnant, inquire about airline policies. Some airlines have restrictions covering passengers during the late stages of pregnancy.

Children 2 and under fly free in the United States and for 10 percent of adult fare on international flights. The child will not be assigned a seat. You can hope for an empty one to use (a good reason to travel at less-favored hours). Otherwise, your child will sit on your lap during the flight as well as for takeoffs and landings. If you do reserve a seat for a child under twelve you will pay between 30% and 50% of the regular adult coach fare though a discounted fare may be more economical. If you're flying alone internationally with two children under 2 years of age, you will have to pay half fare for one of the children, but you will also have a reserved seat for one child.

Many domestic carriers offer reduced fares for children over 2, but ages and offers vary. Airline deregulation has led to a reduction in family fares in general, so it is best to consult a travel agent, who can arrange, by computer, the most economical flight for your family.

> *My daughter was 4 but petite. Since air travel was so expensive, I decided to try to get her on as 2 by holding her and covering her with a blanket. Certainly it was worth a try. I was standing in line in front of the travel agent confirming my seat reservation when the person behind me, apparently taken by my daughter, asked her how old she was. In a loud voice she replied, "I'm 4, but my mother said to say I'm 2."*
>
> Hallie Lerman, Los Angeles, CA

Inquire whether a meal will be served. Some airlines offer special children's meals; request them when making reservations, or at least twenty-four hours before takeoff. If they don't have them, order a fruit plate which is always enjoyable. Order a cold meal for yourself also as you might not know when you'll have the moment to eat and at least your meal won't get cold! Keep in mind that all airline food is prepared by flight kitchens on the ground ahead of time. If you have a fussy eater, bring your own meal or snack.

Although many airlines and travel agents will make reserved seating arrangements by phone, some will not, unless you're traveling first class on a business flight, or, sometimes, if you've reserved a bassinet. However, this system is changing rapidly, and it is best to confirm details with the airline directly.

• Reserve a bassinet ahead of time if you need one and one is available. Be aware that most are only 27 inches long and 12 inches wide, so if your baby is bigger than that or weighs more than 30 pounds, you won't be able to use one.

• Ask the airline what its policy is regarding strollers. Some allow them; others insist they be checked as luggage. A combination stroller/car seat can be removed from its frame and the frame can be checked as you board.

• Select flight times that don't coincide with feeding times, say some travelers, although you'll be nursing or bottlefeeding an infant during takeoff and landing to reduce ear discomfort from changes in air pressure. Others say it's more important to avoid flight times that coincide with naptime.

• Try to avoid peak travel hours in the morning or early evening, when the plane is likely to be full. Putting up with the inconvenience of even a late-night flight may mean that there will be an extra seat for your child, as well as the possibility of more help from airline attendants.

• Ask for a flight that originates in your city (if possible) to ensure better seat selection. They usually depart on schedule.

• Be sure to let them know you're flying with kids so you won't be assigned exit row seats as they will change you once on board.

We waited for our plane at a short stopover, trying to keep tabs on two active children, when I suddenly heard the ear-shattering blast of the airport alarm siren. I dived under the nearest chair, fearing we'd be blown up any minute. I looked frantically for my husband and children. Finally I saw my son standing behind a NO ADMITTANCE sign with his hand on a switch and a "now what do I do?" expression on his face. I walked quickly to the ladies' room and remained there until our plane was called, letting Dad handle the situation.
                                        Gail Dodge, Wilmington, NC

• Choose a nonstop flight when you can, so you won't have to deal with extra landings and take-offs that cause air pressure changes, the hassles of changing planes and waiting in airline terminals. (Alternatively, choose flights that offer extra time between flights rather than cutting it close. That extra airport stopover time gives a mobile child the chance to run and stretch, which fortunately is acceptable airport behavior.)

• Check out plane fares and schedules at this web site: http://www.pctravel.com. It is one of many on-line.

Choosing the Best Seats

• Request the window and aisle seats in a three-seat row if you're traveling with one child (under 2) and another adult, and hope that the middle seat won't be taken. If it is, the occupant will probably be happy to exchange seats so that your family can sit together with your child now on your lap.

• Consider asking for the window seat if you are alone and traveling with an infant. A window seat also offers the most privacy for breast-feeding. Choose the aisle seat if you are alone with a mobile toddler so you won't constantly have to climb over passengers for a trip to the bathroom or some aisle-sightseeing.

• Watch for (or ask an attendant about) rows of empty seats into which your family can move later.

• Ask for seats on the same side of the aisle if you're traveling with two adults and more than one child. Tending children who are in front of or behind you will be easier than reaching across the aisle, which will be impossible while attendants serve food or drinks. Flight rules require one adult per child in a row, in case it's necessary to handle oxygen masks.

• Choose seats away from busy areas such as the galley if you are hoping your child will take a nap.

• Ask for seats at least several rows in front of the smoking section (if there is one) if you are not picking bulkhead seats.

Pros and Cons of
Bulkhead Seats

Many parents feel that seats in the bulkhead are best for traveling with small children. These seats face the walls that separate the different sections of the cabin. They allow room for you to stretch your legs, arrange the children's paraphernalia, or change a non-messy diaper on the floor. A child can't annoy a passenger in front of you—only behind you!

One disadvantage is that the position of meal trays in the bulkhead may make it difficult for you to tend a child as you eat. There is no storage room under the seat in front of you so the attendant will move your carry-on baggage out of your reach during takeoff and landing. Also, the armrests between these seats do not lift up.

If you're traveling on a jumbo jet, the bulkhead seats in the center aisle will be near the lavatories, which means that there may be a line of waiting passengers hovering about you in the aisles. On the bright side, these people may help entertain your child.

Bulkhead seats frequently offer obstructed views of the in-flight movie. Bulkheads in the rear sections may have enough space for kids to play on the floor. These areas on international flights are often in the smoking section, however.

Other parents prefer seats near the rear of the plane. You'll be close to the flight attendants, whose assistance you may need and whose activities may amuse the children.

Bulkhead seats can't always be reserved in advance. You can request them when you arrive for check in. Obviously the earlier you arrive, the better your options are to get the bulkhead (or other) seats.

• Seats in the back on an uncrowded flight can become your playground if you stay out of the attendants' way.

• Be sure the bulkhead seats you get on a jumbo jet are on the center aisle, not by the doors. Small children are not allowed to occupy seats next to these emergency doors, so you'll be required to move if you were inadvertently assigned these seats. (Be aware that some airlines have a limited number of oxygen masks available in the bulkhead area and might not be able to seat families there.)

> *We opted for the "red eye"—the all night flight. The kids slept the whole trip. They were amazingly resilient to jet lag and time changes. The biggest challenge was getting them back on a schedule once we got home.*
> Toni Martin, Sacramento, CA

Using Your Car Seat on the Airplane

Car seats approved by the FAA (Federal Aviation Administration) manufactured after January 1, 1981, except for those which are a vest and harness-type restraint can now be used during takeoff and landing. If you have not paid for a seat for your child under the age of 2, you can use the car seat only if an extra cabin seat is available. If you have brought the car seat on board and there is no extra seat, the flight attendant may stow it for you or, more likely, check it as baggage.

Although it's not mandatory, the FAA recommends using the approved car seat in a window seat for the convenience of the other passengers. It can't be used in the emergency exit access rows or in the rows just in front of and in back of them. The car seat must be properly secured to the passenger seat at all times during the flight, even when your child is not sitting in it.

When on board, the FMVSS label in red lettering, (Federal Motor Vehicle Safety Standard) should be attached to the car seat, indicating make and model number. If the FMVSS sticker is not on it, it may be refused at the gate. It is still wise to check the airline's policies to be sure they will accept a seat with an FMVSS label and whether they will require purchase of a ticket for the car seat's use. The car seat can't be wider than 16 inches.

A 1995 FAA report found that forward-facing safety seats may not safeguard children in a survivable air crash. Rear-facing seats used for children under 20 pounds are effective though seldom used as most airlines let children under age 2 travel free if they sit on an adult's lap. If a child is old enough to ride in a car booster seat, the report said, he or she would be better off just using the adult seat belt on board.

Flight Preparations

If you're taking a stroller, make it a lightweight umbrella stroller. Most fit down the aisles of the plane and usually fit in the overhead bins. Use it to hold your carry on items and have the baby "attached" to you. (Don't be shocked if your airline won't allow any stroller in the cabin. If it's not going to be allowed on it can still be "gate checked" which means since it is last-on luggage and it will be first off at the baggage claim area or can even be brought to the gate when you arrive.

• Read *Going on an Airplane* by Fred "Mr" Rogers (Putnam). With plenty of photos, this book is a good introduction to plane travel. Especially helpful for first-time fliers.

• Arrive at the airport at least fifteen minutes earlier than if you were traveling alone. You'll need the extra time when you have children along. And use this time to make your own run to the toilets. It's more of a challenge once you're in the plane.

• Confirm your seat reservations, if you made them ahead of time, as soon as you arrive. Don't assume the computer is flawless!

• Explain to your toddler that all items, even favorite teddies, must be given up temporarily to pass through the security check, but that they will be returned in just a minute.

• A useful item for carrying a small baby on to a plane is a reclining infant seat with an adjustable stand and handles. Or better yet, carry your baby on in a sling or soft frontpack—or even a backpack.

• In your carry-on luggage, include everything you'll need in case your luggage is lost. Consider putting the contents of your purse into a heavy-duty resealable plastic bag that fits into the flight bag, eliminating one more item to carry.

• Pack your flight/baby bag with one whole day's worth of supplies and clothing for the children and then some. (There is nothing worse than being stranded in soiled clothes, or without enough diapers or formula.)

• Sweatsuits are excellent travel gear for toddlers as well as older children. Every age child should wear socks with their shoes as the floor of a plane is often quite cold.

• Consider taking along a coverall or apron to protect your clothes. That way you don't have to worry about a change of clothes for yourself. (Packing more than one bib for baby is also a good idea.)

Before You Board

• Invest in a flight club membership if you travel a lot on one airline. Flight clubs provide TV's, refreshments and usually a quieter atmosphere.

• Look for specific areas designated as nurseries, now available in many large airports. These are unattended areas near ladies' rooms, with extra space, seating, and a variety of amenities. Some European airport nurseries are supervised, so you can leave your child while you check in.

• Double-diaper or use a nighttime diaper on your baby just before boarding; diaper changing space on a plane is basically nonexistent. If you must make a change on board, use your seat space only if your family is occupying three contiguous seats, or use the floor if you have the bulkhead seats. (Warn your neighboring passengers if you must change a diaper near them.) You can use the toilet lid in the restroom—not easy, but possible. Bring a towel or small piece of folded, washable vinyl to put under the baby for diaper changing. Carry self-sealing plastic bags for dirty diaper disposal.

• Consider bringing your own brown-bag meal. Even though children over 2 are entitled to a meal, that doesn't mean they'll eat it, or that it will come when your child is hungry.

• Bring a lightweight baby blanket with you. It can be used to form a makeshift tent to help cut off visual stimulation if you are trying to get your baby to sleep.

On airplane trips, an umbrella stroller is wonderful. In the bulkhead seat, we can set it up, put the child in it, and have some free hands.
                              Becky Gammons, Beaverton, OR

• Check your baby's car seat with your luggage if you are not going to use it in flight. Be sure to tag it with your name and address. Packing it in a large, heavy-duty plastic garbage bag, while not required, will help protect it.

• Forewarn a child who's old enough to understand that running in the aisles is not allowed and that "playground voices" aren't, either.

• Consider feeding your child before you board when sitting in the departure lounge. A sandwich, a fruit or even an airport meal may keep your child satisfied until the airline meal can be served.

• Let your toddler carry his or her own little flight bag or wear a small backpack with special toys or snacks inside.

• If your flight 's delayed, or you have an unusually long layover in Missoula, Montana, San Jose, Denver, Pittsburgh , Boston or La Guardia in New York, look for a Kidport. These are spaces that offer an excellent place for children to play (although they must be supervised by their parents).

• Entertain a bored child with a long wait to board a plane with a ride on a baggage cart that has a special child's seat. It may well be worth paying even the rental price, if required.

• Keep kids awake before a flight—even help them to wear themselves out—so they'll sleep after take-off.

On Board

• Take advantage of the system that allows parents with small children to board before everyone else. With two children one parent can board early with the carry-ons and the other parent can board last with the more restless child to minimize seat confinement time.

• Help yourself to pillows and a blanket from the overhead luggage rack *before* takeoff, as there probably will not be enough for each passenger if the flight is full.

• Carry an infant in a soft front pack to free your hands. Your baby might be content to be there the whole trip. Make sure the seat belt is over your pelvis and not the baby's during takeoff and landing.

• Remove the armrest between seats (except in the bulkhead, where it's not removable) by raising it to give a child room to stretch out. The flight attendant can help you.

• Put a big bib on your toddler and remove it just before you land if you want to arrive with a clean child. (Or carry "arrival clothes" that you dress the children in after the plane lands.)

• Don't forget to ask the airline attendant for in-flight mementos such as a wing pin, a deck of cards, or a postcard. Ask for these items shortly after takeoff. When the flight attendants get busy, they may not have time to bring them right away.

• Be sure there are airsick bags in your seat pockets. You can use the bags for soiled diapers, too, but be sure to give them to the flight attendant to dispose of properly. Do not leave them in seat pockets when you disembark!

• Be prepared for unusual behavior from your child. The child who always naps may fool you, and your gregarious baby may cry when a stranger acts friendly.

• Don't promise kids a visit to the cockpit during the flight. Do ask your flight attendant before you take off if a trip to the cockpit might be possible after everyone is on board or after you've landed.

• If your flight offers headsets and music, look for a children's music station.

• Use the free air-route map in the seat pocket to track your trip with an older child.

My two-year-old and I were flying to see my parents. He had been playing quietly with his dozen or so Matchbox® cars. The plane began its descent gently but not gently enough to keep those little cars on the tray. Over the top they went, to roll under twelve rows of seats ahead of us. I spent the time before we were ordered to buckle up for landing canvassing the aisle. "Pardon me, sir, but if you look under your seat, I think you'll find..."

Phyllis Anderson, Los Angeles, CA

• Cope with the dry air in planes by getting plenty to drink (not the cola variety), frequent use of Chapstick, or indulging in a face-spray can of mineral water (which kids particularly think is great fun).

Coping with Cabin Pressure Changes

Most ear problems in the air occur when a plane is changing altitudes, especially when it's ascending or descending. Smaller children are more susceptible to discomfort, as the eustachian tubes in their ears are narrower and more prone to collapse with altitude changes. The trick is to keep the jaw working and the saliva flowing to help equalize the pressure.

• Let your baby nurse or suck on a bottle or pacifier during takeoff and landing to reduce pressure on ears. A hungry child will suck more vigorously, so don't feed your baby just before you take off. Babies' sucking reflex can be activated by touching their lips, or having them suck on your finger. Do not allow your baby to sleep during the plane's descent.

• Give gum, chewable mints or lollipops to older children during takeoff and landing.

• Or keep a small cup of water from which to take small sips as cabin pressure changes.

• Try to get your child to yawn, which helps make ears "pop" and relieves pressure, as do other exaggerated facial movements. Make a game of making faces.

• Let a child simply "suck" on a straw without drinking any liquids.

• Or hold a child's nose closed while he or she swallows to "pop" ears open. Several swallows may be necessary.

If air pressure changes cause real ear pain for your child, ask the flight attendant for help. The attendant can provide two styrofoam cups stuffed with hot, moist paper towels to be held over each ear. The steam seems to help reduce the discomfort.

If your child has a cold and must fly, ask your doctor to recommend or prescribe an oral decongestant. Be sure your child sits upright during descent. Be aware that clogged or painful ears are temporary problems but can take as long as three days to return to normal. If your child has problems after that, see a doctor.

In-Flight Nourishment

Remember the old Boy Scout motto "Be Prepared" and don't travel without formula for a bottle-fed baby and snacks for older youngsters. There's always plenty of juice or water on board but the flight's milk supply can run low.

• Ask the flight attendant for water or juice for yourself and your toddler before takeoff or later on. Dry air in the plane can cause a sore or scratchy throat and a dry nose, especially on very long flights. Bring the liquids you need for your baby. Don't expect immediate service when you need it.

• Ask also about the best time to get help with warming the baby's food or bottle, if warming is important to you. (*Babies usually don't care.*)

• The free cola drinks airlines offer contain caffeine, which can "speed up" kids and keep them from sleeping, as well as keep you running to the bathroom with them.

• Remember that bagels are long-lasting, compact, sturdy and basically crumbless snacks.

• Take turns eating when two adults are traveling with a small child (ask the attendant to bring the other meal about 5 minutes later) so one adult has free hands and lap for the child.

• Don't let toddlers eat the airline nut snacks unless you're *sure* there's no chance of choking or aspirating them.

WARNING
**Don't drink any hot beverage when flying
with a small child.
A spilled drink can burn a child—*or you*!**

Those L-o-n-g Flights
• Let an active toddler jog around the airport to tire him- or herself out before boarding the plane.

• Remember that airport gift shops sell a good selection of last-minute games and toys. Look for quiet games designed for travel, but be wary of small pieces that can be lost or swallowed.

• Gift wrap some small toys or favorite munchies and hand them out, one at a time, as a reward for a toddler's good behavior. Pass out these surprises every half hour or so (depending on the length of the flight), but only on the condition that the child continues to play quietly.

• Ask the flight attendant for a sanitary napkin pad to use inside a disposable or cloth diaper to stretch your diaper supply if you think you are running short.

• Help your children space the games and activities they engage in to prevent boredom.

• Don't expect a young child to be entertained for long by in-flight movies or music. Bring a cassette player of your own in case the airline's selection of entertainment doesn't interest your child. The headsets the airlines provide are not always comfortable on the ears. (Remember that radio headsets can't be used because they interfere with the plane's radio transmissions.) If your cassette player can record, all the better; its entertainment value will be expanded.

Anticipating Jet Lag
For some reason that is not well understood, it is easier for people to adjust to a flight going west rather than east. The more time zones you cross, the longer it will take your child to adjust. Changing time zones is a hard adjustment for children and it will take them more than one day to acclimate. Still, the faster you get onto your new time, the faster your body will adjust. A few extra naps may be in order.
• Changing time zones also affects eating schedules. Try demand-feeding your baby for a while until he or she adjusts. Eating schedules will adjust sooner than sleep routines.

• Allow for recovery time when you get to where you are going, but try to adjust to the clock on the wall from the start.

Deplaning
• Accept any help offered.

Keeping our child entertained was our biggest problem. For long car or plane trips with a 1- to 2-year-old, fill an old wallet with expired credit cards, or heavy paper cut to the same size and some cards from an old deck of cards. Our daughter spent several minutes looking at each before throwing it down. Also fill containers with small objects such as shells, small toys, and so on. Picture books and National Geographic kept her attention for long stretches, too.

Barbara Deleebeeck, Stavanger, Norway

With kids 2 and under, be prepared for everything you can think of and then realize that the one thing you haven't thought of will happen. Expect to be embarrassed and, if you hear people mentioning you to their friends in the baggage claim area ("There's the lady with the baby who screamed for forty-five minutes"), take some comfort from the fact that you're not the only one to whom this has happened and that you'll never see these people again!

Sharon Amastae, El Paso, TX

- Take the unused airsick bag for future cleanups.

- Don't feel you have to be first off the plane when you land. Use your judgment. Standing in a hot, crowded aisle with a child or two can ruin your arrival.

- Make a potty stop once you're off the plane and on your way to the baggage claim area. The stalls for the handicapped usually are roomy enough to allow you to bring your child (even one in a stroller) in with you.

- Mark your luggage with distinctive ribbons or stickers so your child can help you spot it quickly as it comes down the conveyor belt.

Kids Traveling Alone By Plane

It is not uncommon to see children traveling by themselves on commercial airliners today. If you are preparing your child for such a trip, approach it as an adventure. Explain, in detail, how he or she will be met at the other end and coach your child on a possible unexpected happening such as ear pain which might occur on takeoff and landing. Provide them with gum or candy to chew and explain how that will relieve the pressure.

Unaccompanied children ages 5 to 7 are usually allowed only on direct flights or if there is a stop with no plane change. (TWA has a minimum age of 7.) Escorts are available for a child if there are connecting flights to make, but there is usually a fee for this service—or actually for each connection. Children 8 to 12 years of age are allowed on any flight but are still considered unaccompanied minors (UM) and must be checked in as such.

When you make your reservations, be sure to indicate if your child is flying as a UM as airlines have specific requirements. The airline is responsible for the child from check-in time until the child is met at his or her final destination. The adult picking up your child will probably need to present a photo I.D. before the airline personnel will release your child.

If travel is to Mexico, Latin or South America, a child must carry notarized permission signed by both parents.

If your child must fly alone, there are some things you can do to make it go smoothly.

• Consider making a visit to the airport in advance of your child's scheduled trip. Point out the departure gate; how to read the arrival/departure monitors; the location of public phones and how to place a call.

• Request a special meal (a children's meal or fruit plate) for your child, but do so at least 24 hours in advance. There's no extra charge.

• Look around the boarding areas for possibly friendly faces who may befriend your child en route or just give a friendly wave when walking down the aisle.

109

• Watch the planes take off and land. Use this as an opportunity to identify and discuss any fears your child may have.

• Talk about details of the flight including what kind of food is served and whether or not a movie may be offered.

On the day of their flight:
• Don't overload your child with heavy carry-on baggage.

• Check in at the airport early. There are forms to fill out with names, addresses and phone numbers for your child, including that of the person who is meeting him or her.

• Check the weather conditions at the destination. A snowed-in airport may not be acceptable for landing. Stay until the flight takes off—just in case it comes back to the terminal for mechanical repairs before take-off   .

• Tell your child to call you upon arrival at the final destination. Make sure you are at home to receive the call. (Does your child know how to call collect or use your phone credit card?)

Train Travel
Train travel often offers spectacular views of the country-side, usually of more interest to adults than to small children. It also allows more freedom of movement than either air or car travel, although if you're on a long trip, you'll find sleeping accommodations cramped. Although it can be pleasant for adults, don't delude yourself—a long train trip with an active toddler can be very wearing.

Though it's fun to explore the bathrooms and the doors of the trains, it's important to encourage caution while walking along the aisles and the bi-level stairways.

Reserving Your Space

Train travel is relatively inexpensive. Amtrak offers family fares that make it even more attractive.

Adults	Full fare. Each adult is allowed 2 children's fare tickets.
Children 2-15	50% off when accompanied by adult
Under 2	50% fare to occupy own seat
Under 2	Free if child sits on adult's lap

Children under the age of 8 may not travel unaccompanied. Ages 8 to 11 may travel unaccompanied under certain conditions and must pay the full fare. Prior written permission is required from the person in charge at the station where you board.

Reservation procedures vary depending on where you're going. On some long-distance routes you can reserve a private compartment for your family. This is an added expense, of course, and you'll have to decide if it's worth it.

Amtrak also offers a variety of family tours including combination rail/sail and air/rail packages. On a limited number of eastern trains, car carriers are included.

For wheelchair assistance call the Special Services Desk at least 24 hours in advance. Special diet menus can be requested if made 72 hours in advance of your trip.

For the specifics of your particular route, brochures, and timetables, call or write: Amtrak Distribution Center, P.O. Box 7717, Itasca, IL 60143; 800-USA-RAIL (800)872-7245) (800)523-6590-TDD, http://www.amtrack.com. From Canada call: (800)426-8725. To travel by passenger train in Canada contact Via Rail Canada at (800)387-1144 (from the U.S.)

• Consider taking a night train and booking a bedroom to get you where you're going while the family sleeps. You will also get complete meals with a bedroom booking (except for Slumbercoach). Request a room that is not over the wheels as that noise may make sleep more difficult.

• Get to the depot early if you haven't reserved a compartment. Your reservations will not be for specific seats, and you'll want to be able to find seats together.

• Try to get seats directly in a row. Many seats face each other or can be turned to do so.

• Check whether a dining car will be available. Most are only on long-distance trains. When available, reserve an early dinner seating with the kids. Snack-bar service is available in the Cafe and Lounge cars on shorter trips. Consider bringing your own snacks and sandwiches to save money and to be sure the food will appeal to your child as the dining room may not work for you.

Other Considerations

• Bring all baby-care items and foods—snacks and drinks—you need with you. You won't be able to buy them on the train. Fruits and vegetables are also hard to come by. Train food is expensive. Dining cars and snack areas are not always open.

• Plan to bring no more luggage than you can handle by yourself. Porters aren't always available. If you do need special assistance, ask the conductor to call ahead for a porter to meet you at the platform. Some Amtrak stations have free luggage carts, but you can't always count on their availability at busy times.

• Take a narrow umbrella stroller so you can walk your baby up and down the aisle.

• Wedge a backpack with a metal frame or stand on a seat to let a child see out the window, or bring your car seat. Either can be used as a booster seat in the dining car.

• Watch your mobile toddler closely. Playing or running

in the aisles is annoying to others—and dangerous. Encourage cautious walking, as rough places in the tracks can throw anyone off balance easily.

• Warm food or formula by putting the container into running hot water in a bathroom basin. Or ask food-service people to warm bottles and baby food for you. Or bring an electric bottle warmer or small hot water coffee pot. (Bathrooms have electrical outlets.)

• You must wear headphones to listen to radios, tape players, or TV's on the train.

• Remember that each passenger car will have a water dispenser.

• Consider carrying your own small towel, washcloth, soap or even toilet paper since every train might not be adequately equipped.

• Because temperatures in trains vary, request pillows and blankets. If you are only on a day trip or sitting in coach all night, these might not be available. Consider bringing your own. Also, dress children in layers of cotton clothes to be prepared for these temperature variations.

• Plan to tip train personnel who are helpful to you.

Bus Travel

Bus travel is sometimes the least expensive kind of public transportation or the only option available, but it's also the most difficult with very young children. Cramped quarters, frequent stops, and a stuffy atmosphere make buses less appealing for everyone concerned, especially on long trips.

All children under the age of 5 must be accompanied by a passenger at least 12 years of age or older. (Greyhound draws the line at 8 for UM traveling alone.) Children ages 5 through 11 traveling unaccompanied, and those age 12 and older are charged the full adult fare. Trips must be no longer than 5 hours long and there can be no change of bus.

Those under 2 travel free on your lap. Kids ages 2 to 4 pay 10% of the adult fare and get a seat. (If you wish a seat for a child under 2, you pay 10% too.) Children under 12, when traveling with a full-fare adult, are charged half the adult fare.

Contact Greyhound passenger service at (800) 231-2222 or check their web site at http://www.greyhound.com/gliservc.html.

• Be prepared to hold your baby on your lap for the entire ride if the bus is full. There are no other accommodations for infants, unless you purchase a second seat. Practice changing your baby in your lap; the bathroom on a bus is too small.

• Bring everything you'll need for the baby in a small bag that's easy to handle. If the bus is crowded, you won't have much room for carry-on luggage.

• Try to get the seats at the front of the bus where your child will be able to see out the windows more easily.

• Pack a transistor radio with headphones to entertain your child. Reception is especially good near the windows.

• Take along food, at least for the children. Meal stops are limited in time and not always at places you would choose.

• Carry your own motion-sickness bag, just in case. Buses don't provide them.

Treat all modes of travel as an adventure—a special occasion. Your attitude and your sense of fun will determine much about the quality of your trip.

Chapter Eight

TRAVELING ABROAD

Traveling abroad with an infant or a small child can be an exciting adventure. The universal appeal of a baby can enhance your trip as much as it complicates it, and many parents have found that their *bambino* has provided an entree for warm experiences. What you lose in romantic evenings you may make up for in friendly encounters. Older children easily find and make friends with local children. Language barriers are seldom a problem for them.

If your budget allows, you may want to consider an *au pair* (usually a student) who will travel with you, help with your child or children, be generally useful, and may even act as an interpreter and guide. There are employment agencies that specialize in placing *au pairs*. European newspapers have ads placed by such young women looking for this type of work. When you do hire a sitter for very young children , don't worry if she doesn't speak English. "*No*" is universal.

Flexibility is again the key. A rested and well-fed child (not to mention parent) is vital to the success of extended travel. Don't get into the trap of "getting your money's worth." When your child needs rest, stop and get yours, too.

Look for a European train feature called the Baby or Family Train (or Cars) which offer special services for families.

Getting Ready to Go

Try to plan for a stay of three to four days in any one place to create a minimum of upheaval in your child's routine. And give yourself at least one day a week without any activity scheduled, just to catch up.

Planes on trans-oceanic flights will carry baby supplies if the airline knows there will be a baby on board, so let them know. These are really meant for emergency use when you run short. Bring what you need with you.

Don't expect anyone else to provide anything for your baby, and you won't be disappointed. Plan ahead, make lists of what you'll need, pack accordingly, and your trip should go smoothly.

Passports and Visas

All U.S. citizens, including infants, must have passports to visit foreign countries (except Canada, Mexico, and some Caribbean islands). Applications for passports are accepted at your local courthouse or at a U.S. Passport Agency office. Passports are valid for 5 years for children under 18, and for 10 years for adults. Passports cost $40 for children under 18, and $65 for adults. Children over 13 must apply personally. For more detailed information check web site: http://travel.state.gov/passport_services.html.

A few countries also require visas. A visa is the official stamp in your passport that allows you to enter a specific foreign country. First, find out if the country you'll be visiting requires one. If it does, apply to the consulate of the country you wish to visit, sending along your passport and a photo. It's usually a relatively simple matter, but it may be more complicated if you are planning a trip to Eastern Europe. Your best bet is to consult a travel agent who is familiar with making these arrangements. For visa information on the Internet go to: http://www.moon.com/tm/tm13/visa.html or www.travel.state.gov/visa_services.html.

When one parent is traveling alone with a child, some countries will not allow the child to cross their border without written permission from the absent parent.

• Make your travel plans early. A passport can take six weeks or longer to process, especially during peak travel times (spring and summer), when many others are applying. It may take a month or more to obtain visas from each country you plan to visit. However, if you are rushed, make the fact known; special arrangements may be possible.

• You can apply for a passport for a child under 13 without having the child present.

• Take certified copies of birth certificates (with a raised stamp imprint) for each family member when applying for passports. Adults will also need a driver's license or other picture identification. Call to see if you'll need anything else.

• Arrange for a passport photographer to take the photographs you will need. Some photo developing shops offer this service. Be sure to find out how many copies you'll need first as visa documents require pictures, too. Call ahead and allow sufficient time for processing. If you don't go to a photographer who specializes in passport photos, be sure you know what rules apply before you have your picture taken by someone else.

• Carry several extra passport photos with you in case you lose your passport or change plans on the journey and need visas for countries not listed in your passport. Keep a record of your passport number and the place and date of its issue in your wallet. If you lose your passport, report this to a U.S. embassy or consulate.

• Photocopy every health record and vital document you might possibly need.

• Leave a detailed itinerary with friends or relatives so you can be reached in an emergency. Give them your passport number and insurance information, too.

• Unlike domestic flights, you must confirm international flights within seventy-two hours of your departure. Don't forget. You run the risk of losing your reservation.

Listen to Uncle Sam

The US State Department operates a 24-hour recorded hotline with advice on everything from terrorist threats to disease concerns around the world. To hear information on the specific area you are traveling to, call (202)647-5225 for the latest information. It can also be accessed on the Internet at: http://travel.state.gov/travel_warnings.html.

Car Rentals Abroad

While driving can be a terrific way to travel, it's important to keep certain differences in mind. In countries where lanes are "reversed", be very careful. Your automatic reflex to turn the "wrong way" must be overcome. Also, drinking and driving offenses carry more serious consequences in other countries than they do in the US.

• Keep in mind that car labels such as "intermediate size" don't necessarily mean the same abroad as they do here. Also, gas and toll prices are higher than in the U.S.

• Make arrangements as far ahead as possible and have any reservation confirmed in writing. (This applies to hotels as well.) Ask about any additional taxes or costs. Ask which credit cards they accept. Round-trip rentals are less expensive than one-way rentals.

• Rental cars can be targets for street thieves abroad. Don't leave your belongings on the seats in plain view.

• Bring your infant car seat if you'll be traveling by car. Be sure it's an FAA-approved model so you can also use it on the airplane. Many foreign car-rental agencies don't have them, and the ones that do often will not allow you to make one-way rentals. Avis (800-331-1212), Hertz (800-654-3131), Budget (800-527-0700), and National (800-328-4567) have car seat rentals available in some cities. Check when you make your overseas car-rental reservations.

Other Reliable Overseas Auto Rentals

AutoEurope   Kemwel
PO Box 1097   106 Calvert Street
Camden, ME 04843   Harrison, NY 10528
(800) 223-5555   (800) 678-0678

Accommodations

Just as in the States, many hotels offer special rates that include children. For information on the Sofitel and Novotel chain in France, call their American representative, Resinter, at (800)221-4542. And check out home rentals and swaps.

119

Most hotel rooms abroad accommodate 2 and sometimes 3 people. For 4 or more look for apartment hotels.

Bring along an American Express credit card as well as your Visa or Master Charge card. AmEx Travel and Money Services in major cities are sometimes only available to you as a cardcarryer and those services often come in handy.

Internet Conversion Sites

For time zone conversion, go to site:
http://poisson.ecse.rpiedu/cgi-bin/tzconvert.

To convert the value of any currency go to site:
http://www.xe.net/currency.

Essentials

• Bring a soft-carrier, frame backpack or a collapsible stroller for sightseeing. These items can be carried aboard the plane. But in some countries (including ours), strollers will not always be allowed in public places such as museums.

Diaper Metrics

Know your baby's weight in kilos if you want to buy the right size. Disposable-diaper sizes are determined by weight, which in most countries is measured in kilos, not pounds.

1 Kilo   = 2.2 Pounds
10 Kilos = 22 Pounds

Proctor and Gamble, at (800)543-0480, will tell you if Pampers/Luvs disposable diapers are sold in the country you plan to visit.

• Pack plenty of disposable diapers—perhaps an entire duffel bag or soft-sided suitcase full—unless you're prepared to make do with whatever you can get. Although some American brands of disposables are available abroad, you may not be able to find them at your location. European disposables are more expensive, and some are simply thick cotton pads designed to fit into rubber pants. American disposables are available but finding them on your route may be difficult. The quality of different types varies, so be prepared to experiment.

• Taking a compact, portable baby crib can be worth the effort. It offers a child a familiar place to sleep every night.

• Bring children's clothes that can be washed in a hotel sink and drip-dried overnight. As in this country, laundromats are available too, and many places will also fold your laundry. Drop off dirty laundry in the morning and pick it up later that day or the next morning.

• Pack lightweight clothing that can be layered—both for temperature control and laundry control.

• Don't forget your own mild soap and a washcloth; not all places provide them. Also carry along a good supply of small sample-size toiletries. You won't find them abroad.

• Pack a mild soap such as Ivory to help prevent diaper rash or irritation from harsh soaps used to launder clothes. Baby shampoo makes an excellent "make-do" detergent.

• Take a roll of soft toilet paper with the center core removed (so it takes up less room) for a multitude of uses, from cleaning bottoms to wiping runny noses. And, of course, don't forget pre-moistened towelettes.

In England many hotels offer something called "baby listening." There are intercoms in all the rooms, and if you request it, while you are in the dining room, at the pool, or elsewhere, someone will listen for your child to awaken, and notify you. When this service is not available, you can take the phone off the hook and the operator will listen for the baby.

Mary McNamara, Wayzata, MN

Medical Matters

Immunizations are not required for travel to Europe, the Soviet Union, Japan, and many other countries. However, if you will be visiting some South American, Asian, or central African countries, it's advisable to be vaccinated against cholera and yellow fever. It's also a good idea to check with your pediatrician to make sure the children are up to date on their regular immunizations.

If you have a choice, it is wise to wait until your child is at least 18 months old before you travel abroad. By then your child will have been immunized against the major childhood diseases, including polio, outbreaks of which have been reported recently in Central and South America. If a small child contracts a serious disease (malaria, for instance), it is much harder to treat given the choice of medicines available for use with a small child. Breast-feeding a baby doesn't protect against these serious diseases.

Preventive inoculations or vaccinations for cholera and yellow fever are not recommended for infants under 6 months. Injections for typhoid can be given after 6 weeks of age but usually cause severe reactions. Protection against certain types of malaria can be given to any baby. All of these need to be given at least 10 days before departure.

For the most current information from the U.S. government's publication, "Health Information for International Travel" contact your local branch of the Public Health Service.

• Discuss with your pediatrician any medical problems your child may have that could cause difficulties while traveling. Ask for recommendations about diet or motion sickness.

• Have a pre-trip checkup, particularly for ears and throat.

• Get the generic names of medications you may need to purchase abroad. Brand names will vary. You will find that many drugs available only by prescription here can be bought over the counter abroad.

• Remember to carry all prescription drugs in their original containers when traveling out of the country, or you may run into trouble at customs. Also bring copies of the prescriptions. Keep them in your carry-on luggage so you'll still have them if your other luggage is lost.

• Inquire at the American Embassy, consulate, a large hotel or Tourist Bureau for names of English-speaking physicians in that country. Since English is frequently the language most doctors are trained in, you probably will not have a problem being understood in most situations

Precautions Against the "Runs"

Stomach upsets abroad usually are caused by bacteria and organisms that are different from the ones our bodies are used to. The problem generally is the result of changes in the water supplies and/or the use of different fertilizers from country to country, but stomach upsets can occur from place to place within countries as well.

Medical Help Services

IAMAT (International Association for Medical Assistance to Travelers), 736 Center St., Lewiston, NY 14092, (716) 754-4883, can give you names of English-speaking physicians, and locations of hospitals in 450 cities and 550 countries. They also provide information on climate, sanitation, and immunization laws.

The following companies offer health insurance, medical evacuation for travelers, or other services which need to be purchased *before* departure. For information, contact:

Access America	(800)284-8300
Europe Assistance	(800)821-2828
Wallach & Co. Ins.	(800)237-6615

When traveling abroad, diarrhea is a real health concern. It is inconvenient at best, and it can be serious, especially in very young children, because it can lead to dehydration. This can be critical with a child under the age of 6 months, and it certainly needs to be watched carefully with a child under the age of 12 months. If your child has five or more watery bowel movements a day for three or more days in a row, get medical attention. If the diarrhea occurs in conjunction with other symptoms (fever, for example), consult a doctor as soon as possible.

Bring your own thermometer along if you are not good at converting Celsius to Fahrenheit.

Foods to avoid: tap water, ice, unpasteurized milk and dairy products, raw vegetables, raw peeled or cut up fruits, raw or undercooked meat, poultry, eggs or seafood, custards, mayonnaise, and dressings.

Foods usually safe to eat: boiled water, bottled water, carbonated beverages, beer, wine hot coffee or tea, refrigerated hard-cooked eggs you peel yourself, hot food served hot, cold food served cold and thick-skinned fruit which can be peeled.

• Be careful about drinking unchlorinated tap water in any country, and do not drink it in Latin America, Asia, or Africa. Remember that this warning applies to ice cubes and water used for brushing teeth. Most European cities have safe drinking water on tap. A good rule of thumb is always to drink bottled water in villages or rural areas.

• Don't let children swallow bath or shower water.

• Bring along a supply of water purification tablets. Or boil water for ten to fifteen minutes to purify it. A heating coil with the proper electrical adapter can be very useful for this purpose.

• Eat only foods that are cooked and peeled, if the quality of food is at all questionable.

• Bring powdered milk and/or formula (even if you are nursing—*just in case*) and mix it with bottled water only. It's a good idea to bring along enough ready-to-serve formula until you can find a reliable source of bottled water.

• Drink only milk and milk products that have been pasteurized. Boxed, unrefrigerated milk is common outside the United States and is safe to drink. It needs refrigeration only after opening, and it tastes like fresh milk.

• Bottled carbonated drinks are safe because the carbonation makes them too acidic for bacteria to survive.

• If drinking water is not chlorinated, odds are that the swimming pool will present the same problem.

• Check with a local American travel bureau to find

restaurants known to prepare foods safe to eat. And keep in mind that most large hotels catering to American tourists are usually safe.

Dealing with Diarrhea

Even if it isn't serious, diarrhea can spoil your fun with diaper leaks, extra laundry, and bathroom-hopping. The best cure is to slow down, curtail activities, and give the body a chance to recover.

Over-the-counter drugs are not recommended for treating diarrhea in children. De-fizzed 7-Up sometimes helps, and is widely available. Cola drinks help too, but keep in mind that they contain caffeine.

Pepto-Bismol has proven effective for some, either taken daily as a preventive measure or to relieve symptoms when they occur, but it is not recommended for small children. Ask your pediatrician to suggest medication before you go.

Home Remedy for a Run-of-the-Mill Case of the *"Runs"*

Mix one 3-ounce package of flavored gelatin with one cup of water and have your child drink as much as he or she can. The gelatin is a good binder, and the sweet taste encourages consumption. Not all countries carry this American staple so you may wish to bring a box or two with you.

The worst side effect of diarrhea is dehydration. Replace lost fluids and electrolytes by drinking apple and orange juices with a pinch of salt added, or tea made with safe boiled water with a bit of baking soda added.

• Encourage drinking of any safe liquids. Breast-fed babies should continue to be breast-fed.

• Eliminate solid food from the diet and switch to skim milk, or better yet, no milk, for a while. Ease back into a normal diet with bananas, applesauce or toast—easy binding foods. Rice is always good and so is water that rice is cooked in.

Food for Thought

• Bringing a hanging portable high chair for eating in restaurants can be helpful, or be prepared to use your stroller, car seat, or lap—which of course is just fine. In Europe and Latin America especially, restaurants do not cater to babies. You'll find sidewalk cafes are more accommodating to children.

• Be prepared for the idiosyncrasies of foreign shopping. For example, in some countries powdered milk is available only in pharmacies, not in grocery stores.

• If you're breast-feeding, be aware that attitudes toward nursing in public are far more relaxed in most foreign countries than in the United States.

• Carry a box of instant baby cereal with you. It is very light in weight and you probably will not find your brand abroad.

• Availability of baby food and baby supplies varies widely from country to country. Before you leave, accustom your child to eating table foods pureed in a baby food grinder.

• If your baby will eat only commercial baby food, bring your own emergency supply.

• Bring along a small can opener or Swiss Army knife. In some countries, you will find only canned baby food.

• Bring a good supply of peanut butter if your child is addicted to it. It's usually not as widely available in many countries as it is here.

Buying Infant Formula Abroad

If you don't pack your own infant formula, be aware that availability of familiar brands varies greatly from country to country. The three major American companies that make infant formula (Ross Laboratories, Mead Johnson, and Wyeth Labs) all distribute their products overseas, usually under the same product names. (One exception is Similac, which is sold as Multival in Germany.) The ingredients may vary slightly depending on local requirements. (Call a children's clinic, pediatrician, or pharmacist at your destination if you're concerned about this.) Most formula sold abroad is in the form of powder, which is less convenient, but more economical. Remember to mix the formula with bottled or boiled water only. The metric system won't pose a problem; just use the scoop provided as you normally would.

If you can't find the formula you want and you don't want to try what's available, call the American embassy and ask if you can shop in their store. Chances are they'll have your brand in liquid form.

• Bring packets of instant cocoa to mix with boiled water as one way to provide your child with calcium.

• Fast-food restaurants (other than a few American chains) are practically nonexistent in Europe. Children's menus are also rare. You can sometimes ask for a smaller portion for a child, for which you will usually pay less than full price.

• Plan to eat your main meal at noon. This is a tradition in many countries, anyway. Many restaurants don't welcome children at their evening meals, which are often long and leisurely and may begin very late.

• Ask your concierge for a good place to dine with children.

• Always have more supplies (food or diapers) for your child than you expect to need. One extra day's worth is often enough. And stock up before weekends, because store hours may be very limited.

Customs and Countries

Don't go with the attitude that only familiar American products will do for you and your child. Explore stores and try their wares. Some folks purposely "forget" items such as toothpaste so they can purchase local products that also are souvenirs to bring home. Think of your trip as educational and none of this will feel frustrating. In most foreign countries tipping is obligatory or expected in public restrooms. Have small change (in local currency) ready. If you must, a US dollar bill will do. But, don't leave quarters, etc. because banks will not exchange these for local currency.

Teach older children how to say simple phrases such as "*please*," "*thank you*," and "*excuse me*" in the language of the country you will be visiting. There are junior Berlitz courses in most major US cities and they have introductory tapes for Spanish and French for prior-to-trip preparation.

Keep a phrase book on hand at all times if you can't speak the language. Using picture flash cards can be helpful for communicating without words. If you need something and don't know the right word, you can show someone a picture of it—primitive, but it works. Still, pointing and gesturing are universal languages everywhere.

Plan to make your own fun outdoors with your children in European parks. Playgrounds equipped with swings, seesaws, and such are very rare

• The word abroad for restroom is *toilet*. If you ask for a bathroom you will be directed to shower or bath. Another common term is W.C. (water closet).

• Be prepared for public rest rooms that are not as clean or well equipped as the ones you're used to. You may be expected to pay for toilet paper, which is of inferior quality. Carrying your own supply of individual tissue packages is a good solution, if not a necessity.

• Carry disposable toilet seat covers with you if you worry about hygiene in out-of-the-way places.

• Purchasing phone tokens rather than using local coins is common in many countries.

Remember that while car rental in Europe may be convenient, a Eurailpass and a Eurail Youthpass (good in sixteen countries) are more economical. Children under age 4 travel free; children under 12 pay half fare. Where reserved seats are required, this pass doesn't guarantee you a seat, so check into each train's requirements. If you will not be doing a lot of multi-country travel, even Eurail may not be your best bet. For train travel in England, Scotland, and Wales, you will need a BritRail pass. These passes can't be purchased in Europe. You must buy them before you leave home. Your travel agent will order them for you. (Also, ask about Eurotrain passes for children and students which can be purchased only in Europe.)

Europe by Train

Send for a free copy of *Eurail Traveler's Guide* which contains a map and *Eurail Timetable* from: Eurailpass, Box 10383, Stamford, CT 06904-2383. Their web site address is: http://www.eurail.com

If you live in Canada write to:
Eurailpass, Box 300, Sauccursale R, Montreal H2S 3K9

Read before you go. Look for *Innocents Abroad: Traveling With Kids in Europe* by Laura Sutherland and Valerie Deutsch (Plume/Viking, 1991), for specific accommodations for families in major cities of 14 countries. Another book on the subject, Fielding's *Europe with Children* by Leila Hadley (Wm Morrow, 1984), contains in-depth information on traveling with kids in 20 European countries, but is now available only in libraries. Also recommended is *Adventuring With Children: An Inspirational Guide to Travel and The Outdoors* by NanJeffrey (Avalon House, 1996).

Bon Voyage!

Hotels and Motels in Canada
when calling within Canada

Coast Hotels	(800) 663-1144*
CP Hotels	(800) 268-9420 Ont./Que.
	(800) 268-9411 Other provinces
	(800) 828-7447 from U.S. only
Days Inn	(800) 344-3636*
Delta Hotels	(800) 268-1133*
	(800) 877-1133 from U.S.only
First Canada	(800) 267-7899
Hilton	(800) 268-9275
Holiday Inns	(800) 465-4329*
Hotel des Gouverneurs	(800) 463-2820 Quebec*
Howard Johnson Hotels	(800) 654-2000*
Hyatt Hotels	(800) 228-9000*
Journey's End Motels	(800) 668-4200*
Marriott	(800) 228-9290*
Radisson	(800) 333-3333*
Ramada Canada	(800) 268-8998
Relax Inns	(800) 661-9563*
Sheraton	(800) 325-3535*
York-Hanover Hotels	(800) 268-1444

Car Rentals

Avis	(800) 268-2310
Budget	(800) 268-8900
Hertz	(800) 263-0600
Thrifty	(800) 367-2277*

* These 800 numbers can be reached from the U.S. *and* Canada.

MUSEUMS TO INTEREST CHILDREN

Boston
Children's Museum of Boston
300 Congress St.
Boston, MA 02210
(617) 426-6500

Museum of Science
Science Park
Boston, MA 02114-1099
(617) 723-2500

Brooklyn
Brooklyn Children's Museum
145 Brooklyn Ave.
Brooklyn, NY 11213
(718) 735-4400

Charlotte
Discovery Place
301 North Tryon St.
Charlotte, NC 28202
(704) 372-6261

Chicago
Chicago Children's Museum
435 East Illinois St.
Chicago, IL 60611
(312) 527-1000

Museum of Science
and Industry
5700 S Lake Shore Dr.
Chicago, IL 60637
(312) 684-1414

Cincinnati
Children's Museum, Cincinnati
700 W. Peter Rose Way
Cincinnati, OH
(513) 421-5437

Denver
Children's Museum of Denver
2121 Crescent Drive
Denver, CO 80211
(303) 433-7444

Houston
Children's Museum of Houston
1500 Binz St.
Houston, TX 77019
(713) 522-1138

Indianapolis
Children's Museum of Indianapolis
3000 North Meridian St.
Indianapolis, IN 46208
(317) 924-5431

Las Vegas
Children's Museum
833 Las Vegas Blvd North
Las Vegas, NV
(702) 382-5437

Los Angeles
Los Angeles Children's Museum
310 North Main Street
Los Angeles, CA 90012
(213) 687-8801

Miami
Miami Youth Museum
5701 Sunset Drive
Miami, FL 33143
(305) 661-2787

New Orleans
Louisiana Children's Museum
428 Julia Street
New Orleans, LA 70130
(504) 586-0725

New York City
Children's Museum of Manhattan
212 W. 83rd St. (Tisch Bldg.)
New York, NY 10024
(212) 721-1234

Children's Museum of the Arts
72 Spring Street
New York, NY 10012
(212) 274-0986

Staten Island Children's Museum
1000 Richmond Terrace
Staten Island, NY 10301
(718) 273-2060

Phoenix
Arizona Museum of Science and
 Technology
147 E. Adams
Phoenix, AZ 85004
(602) 256-9388

Philadelphia
Please Touch Museum
210 North 21st Street
Philadelphia, PA 19103
(215) 963-0667

Pittsburgh
Pittsburgh Children's Museum
One Landmarks Square
Allegheny Center
Pittsburgh, PA 15212
(412) 322-5058

Portland
Children's Museum
3037 Southwest Second Ave
Portland, OR 97201
(503) 823-2227

Salt Lake City
Children's Museum of Utah
840 West 300 North
Salt Lake City, UT 84103
(801) 322-5268

San Francisco
San Francisco Exploratorium
3601 Lyon Street
San Francisco, CA 94123
(415) 563-7337

California Academy of Science
Golden Gate Park
San Francisco, CA 94118
(415) 221-5100

Seattle
The Children's Museum
Seattle Center/305 Harrison
Seattle, WA 98109
(206) 441-1767

Museum of History & Industry
2700 24th Ave East
Seattle, WA 98112
(206) 324-1126

St. Louis
Magic House
516 South Kirkwood Road
St. Louis, MO 63122
(314) 822-8900

St. Paul/Minneapolis
Children's Museum
7th & Wabasha
St. Paul, MN 55101
(612) 225-6000

Science Museum of Minnesota
30 East 10th Street
St. Paul, MN 55101
(612) 221-9488

Tampa
Children's Museum of Tampa
7550 North Boulevard
Tampa, FL 33604
(813) 935-8441

Tuscon
Tucson Children's Museum
200 South Sixth Avenue
Tucson, AZ 85701
(602) 884-7511

Washington, D.C.
Capital Children's Museum
800 3rd St. NE
Washington, D.C. 20002
(202)543-8600

Discovery Creek
4954 MacArthur Blvd NW
Washington, DC
(202) 364-3111

Index

S

safety   48, 71, 91
Safety Belt Song   67
Safety Belt Safe USA   66
seat protectors   67
shopping   41
shopping centers   76-77
short car trips   75
SingAlongSongs for Kids   40, 138
SingAlongTravel Songs   86, 138
sleeping arrangements   42-45
snacks   61, 63, 112
soap   121
souvenirs   41
stroller   28, 127
suite hotels   15
syrup of ipecac   33, 48

T

tantrums   71-77
tapes   40, 86
thirst   55-56
Thrifty Car Rental   132
time zones   100
toddlers   3
toilet facilities   129
toilet paper   121, 129
toilet-seat adapter   32, 138
toys   34-37, 90
train travel   110-113
travel agencies   7
travel games   38-39
travel library   38
Travel Resources   7
TravelWithYourChildren (TWYCH)   7

U

U.M. (unaccompanied minor)   109
U.S. and Worldwide Travel
   Accommodations Guide   19
U.S. Forest Service   88
US State Dept. hotline   118

V

Vacation Exchange Club   17
Villa Leisure   17
Vistatours   7

W

W.C. (water closet)   139
Wallach & Co. Ins   124
weather information   22
Wee Sing song books   40
wheelchair assistance   111

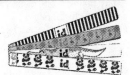